T5-BYV-811

BOOK ILLUSTRA~
TIONS FROM SIX
CENTURIES *in* THE
LIBRARY OF THE
STERLING AND
FRANCINE CLARK
ART INSTITUTE

BOOK ILLUSTRATIONS FROM SIX CENTURIES IN THE LIBRARY OF THE STERLING & FRANCINE CLARK ART INSTITUTE

Essay by Susan Roeper ❧ *Catalogue by Sarah Scott Gibson, Susan Roeper, and J. Dustin Wees*

STERLING AND FRANCINE CLARK ART INSTITUTE ❧ WILLIAMSTOWN, MASSACHUSETTS
1990

This catalogue is published on the occasion of an exhibition at the Sterling and Francine Clark Art Institute, Williamstown, Massachusetts, 28 July to 23 September 1990.

Book design by Jonathon Nix, using Garamond type with Basilea titles.
Typesetting and printing on Mohawk Superfine paper by The Studley Press, Dalton, Massachusetts.

All the photographs were taken by Arthur Evans, Clark Art Institute Photo Facility.

ISBN 931102-29-4

Library of Congress Cataloging-in-Publication Data:

Sterling and Francine Clark Art Institute. Library.
    Book illustrations from six centuries in the Library of the
    Sterling and Francine Clark Art Institute / essay by Susan Roeper:
    catalogue by Sarah Scott Gibson, Susan Roeper, J. Dustin Wees.
        p.   cm.
    Exhibition held July 28-Sept. 23, 1990.
    Includes bibliographical references and index.
    ISBN 0-931102-29-4 (paper)
    1. Illustration of books—Exhibitions. 2. Sterling and Francine
Clark Art Institute. Library—Exhibitions. I. Roeper, Susan,
1957-   . II. Gibson, Sarah Scott. III. Wees, J. Dustin, 1944-
IV. Title.
NC961.W55S747   1990
741.6'4'0747441—dc20   90-9992

COVER: *Maillol woodcut from Longus,* Daphnis & Chloé, *cat. no. 42.*
TITLE PAGE: *Woodcut from Colonna,* Hypnerotomachie, *cat. no. 4.*
PAGE 6: *Diderot,* Encyclopédie, *detail, cat. no. 15.*
PAGE 10: *Goethe,* Faust, *detail, cat. no. 28.*

Alice was beginning to get very tired of sitting by her

sister on the bank, and of having nothing to do: once

or twice she had peeped into the book her sister was

reading, but it had no pictures or conversations in it,

"and what is the use of a book," thought Alice,

"without pictures or conversations?"

LEWIS CARROLL

Alice's Adventures in Wonderland

Fig. 2

FOREWORD

THE INSTITUTE'S COLLECTION OF RARE BOOKS has been largely hidden until now, since it really has no separate place or existence within our considerable research library. Books have been shown and loaned from the collection and additions made to it through gift and purchase, but it has never been the subject of a special exhibition.

There are other good reasons for holding such a show at this time. First and foremost, our Assistant Librarian, Susan Roeper, has recently completed a master's thesis for the University of Chicago on Robert Sterling Clark as a collector of rare books. Secondly, more material has come to light and been published in recent years on Clark as a collector of paintings, and her introductory essay complements this research. Finally, 1990 is the thirty-fifth anniversary of the museum, and, by a happy coincidence, we have just purchased Goethe's *Faust* with Delacroix's remarkable illustrations. This is our first major example of early Romantic lithography and a reminder of the importance of the rare book collection.

About three-quarters of the books in this exhibition were bought by Clark. He seems to have collected them with the same relish and enthusiasm that he brought to the acquisition of other works of art. He liked to spend much time with the dealers discussing the trade and its vagaries. His book buying was launched during the same heady decade in Paris (1911-1921) when the painting collection began to take shape and some of his finest drawings were purchased.

In her introduction, Susan Roeper discusses Clark's individuality as a book collector and quotes his own assessment of himself as such. There are echoes here, of course, of his approach to the collecting of paintings, where subject matter and fineness of execution were of considerable importance, and where if he did not care for someone's work (whatever its importance or art historical significance) he simply didn't collect it. His interests in costume, in horsemanship, and in military matters also appear among his paintings.

Clark was as great a reader of books as he was an examiner of paintings and he often made notes on what he read. We find him "tackling" Rabelais with some gusto, "deep in the *Heptameron*," and finding Montaigne's Journals "a perfect treat." A very private man, he seems to have relished the absorption of a book, and we should note in passing the several readers—and a bibliophile—who appear in his paintings.

I am most grateful to Sarah Gibson, J. Dustin Wees, and especially Susan Roeper for all the care and enthusiasm they have devoted to preparing this exhibition. As members of our library staff they have been rightly concerned with bringing an unfamiliar and very important aspect of the Institute's collection before the public.

David S. Brooke
DIRECTOR

ACKNOWLEDGMENTS

MANY PEOPLE AT THE CLARK ART INSTITUTE have provided much-needed guidance and assistance. We are particularly grateful to David Brooke, Director, for his support; Paige Carter, Catalogue Librarian, for producing the index; Linda Lloyd, Library Secretary, for typing the manuscript; Mary Jo Carpenter, Director of Membership and Public Relations, for overseeing the catalogue's production; and Paul Dion, Preparator, for his careful installation of the exhibition.

Since our research took us to other libraries, we would like to acknowledge the able assistance provided by Mrs. Inge Dupont, Superviser of the Reading Room, The Pierpont Morgan Library, and the staff of Houghton Library, Harvard University. We would also like to thank Robert Volz, Custodian, Chapin Library, Williams College, both for his advice and for his editing of the manuscript with patience and wisdom. And finally, we are indebted to the late Professor Robert Rosenthal of the University of Chicago for his encouragement during the preparation of the thesis that formed the basis of the introductory essay which follows.

S.S.G.

S.R.

J.D.W.

ROBERT STERLING CLARK: A COLLECTOR'S PURSUIT

In the past thirty-five years the public has come to know the collections of paintings, sculpture, prints, drawings, silver, and decorative arts formed by Robert Sterling Clark and his wife, Francine Clark. However, there remains one aspect of the Clarks' art collections which has yet to adorn the galleries, namely the collection of illustrated, finely bound, and rare books formed by Robert Sterling Clark. To be sure, books from this collection have been exhibited on occasion, but never before has the collection itself been the focal point of an exhibition in the main galleries.

Unlike his other collections, Clark's books are no longer housed under one roof. The Library of the Sterling and Francine Clark Art Institute is keeper of the Robert Sterling Clark Collection of rare books which numbers some 1,600 titles. In addition, Yale University's Beinecke Library houses the Robert Sterling Clark Collection of Books on Horses and Military History which contains some 1,100 titles. In Lexington, Kentucky, the library of the Thoroughbred Club of America was initiated through Clark's gift of his collection of racing manuals and stud books. Together, these collections represent perhaps one-half of what Clark acquired in his lifetime.

Clark's collecting activities are recorded in his unpublished diaries and personal correspondence, from which all of the quotations appearing on the following pages were culled. Because Clark kept records of his library in the form of packing lists, appraisals, and receipts for purchases, it has been possible to examine, in particular, the itemized receipts issued by the firms of James F. Drake, Inc., and Bernard Quaritch, Ltd. From these two firms alone, Clark purchased approximately 3,000 books between 1916 and 1954: notably books on horsemanship, illustrated books from the fifteenth through the nineteenth centuries, costume books, and literary first editions. That Clark purchased from other dealers is certain, for less than half of the titles housed at the Clark can be traced to Drake or Quaritch. However, it is reasonably certain that the three collections mentioned above, together with the evidence of titles acquired through Drake or Quaritch but not presently accounted for, provide a clear picture of Clark's activity as a book collector. Because it has not been possible to determine the fate of the remainder of Clark's books, one can only speculate that they were given away in small portions, or, as in the case of the Yale collection, sold.

The Robert Sterling Clark Collection of Books on Horses and Military History was presented to Yale University in 1961 by H. P. Kraus, who said at that time that "it would be impossible to duplicate such a collection, even without regard to cost."[1] In his autobiography, Kraus recounts his purchase of a collection of books on horses from a Parisian bookseller who knew only that the previous owner was "an American turfman who had been living for many years in Paris."[2] Kraus later discovered Clark's identity from bills inserted in some of the books.

Clark had settled in Paris by 1911, where, as is evident in letters to his brother Stephen Clark and to friends in Cooperstown, New York, between the years 1911 and 1916, he spent a good deal of time studying Arabic and Spanish and taking lessons in boxing and horsemanship. It was also during these years that Clark became intent on building a collection of books on "that noble animal, the horse."

In addition to taking lessons in horsemanship, Clark was reading all he could find on the subject. In October 1915, he wrote to a friend that "even my literature consists of reading about whether you pull the right rein or the left one . . . in fact I am rapidly graduating to the stage—longed for by all true horsemen—where I can bore people with a six-hour conversation." Further evidence from his letters suggests that in such a conversation Clark would ponder the "'pince delicat des sperons' of La Guerinière, the 'flexicons' of Baucher, the 'rênes allemandes' of Newcastle [and] the post of Pluvinel."

Before long, his quest for edification began to acquire characteristics more commonly associated with the collector's quest. In January of 1916 he wrote to the same friend, rationalizing his book collecting by musing, "As it is not a thing everyone is interested in, it is not too expensive a habit." Illustrating his point, Clark mentions his purchase of Federico Grisone's *Ordini di cavalcare* (Venice, 1590) for four dollars. But, he continues, "I will not say the same for Monsieur de Pluvinel . . . which is sought after by other than horsemen on account of its engravings, but then there are only two or three books of this sort of thing which are worth anything much from the collector's point of view."

Clark was referring to Antoine de Pluvinel's *Maneige royal* (Paris, 1623), with plates designed and engraved by Crispijn de Passe II. By 1919 Clark was willing to purchase the 1629 edition of this work, published under the title *L'instruction du roy* and containing the same plates. He also acquired the 1625 edition (cat. no. 7), issued with the same plates and the first text faithful to Pluvinel's manuscript. Also in 1919 Clark returned the Venice 1563-1565 edition of Grisone, sent on approval by Quaritch, perhaps because he found a copy of the Pesaro edition of 1558 bearing the gilt arms of Cardinal Hippolyte d'Este and containing marginal notes identified as being in the handwriting of Torquato Tasso. He also found the same title translated into German (Augsburg, 1570) containing very fine woodcut illustrations erroneously attributed to Jost Amman (cat. no. 6).

Clark continued to acquire equestrian treatises by horsemen such as Sir Nicholas Malbie and Gervase Markham throughout his lifetime. Among the notable additions to his collection was the Huth library copy of the very rare *Art de chevalerie* by Jean Jacques de Wallhausen (Frankfurt, 1616), which Clark acquired in 1920. As late as 1932 he acquired the first edition of Peter Beckford's *Thoughts on Hunting* (London, 1781), which Ernest R. Gee, in *The Sportsman's Library*, calls the "corner-stone of a huntsman's library."[3] But by this time the majority of horse books purchased by Clark were those considered valuable "on account of their engravings" or otherwise fine illustrations.

As the nineteenth century was Clark's favorite artistic era, it is not surprising that he sought books illustrated by the renowned sporting artists Henry Alken and John Leech. Clark initially sought those illustrated by Alken, the more prolific, making his first purchase in 1921. The book was C. J. Apperley's novel *The Life of a Sportsman* (London, 1842), with thirty-six colored aquatints (cat. no. 31). Clark continued to buy Alken-illustrated works throughout the decade, including his ambitious folio *The National Sports of Great Britain* (London, 1821) and, from the Jerome Kern sale in 1929, a panorama [*Going to Epsom Races . . .*, n.d.] mounted on rollers in a mahogany box with a glass top. Also in 1929 Clark purchased *Jorrocks's Jaunts and Jollities* (London, 1843) by the novelist Robert Smith Surtees, with fifteen colored aquatints by Alken.

While Alken was given credit for the success of Surtees's sporting classics, it was John Leech who would, in the words of Gordon Ray, "realize the possibilities of Mr. Jorrocks as a character" and establish him as "one of the half dozen most memorable figures in the pantheon of Victorian illustration."[4] The book responsible for this assessment is Surtees's *Handley Cross, or, Mr. Jorrocks's Hunt* (London, 1854). Mr. Clark would likely concur with Ray's opinion, for during the 1930s he sought books illustrated by Leech and, with one exception, ceased to buy those illustrated by Alken. While there is no evidence that *Handley Cross* numbered among Clark's books, Clark did acquire two of the four other books produced by the partnership of Leech and Surtees. In 1930 he had, on approval from Drake, six of Leech's original drawings for Surtees's *Mr. Sponge's Sporting Tour*. He declined to purchase these but in 1934 bought the published edition (London, 1853) with a total of thirteen hand-colored etchings and eighty-nine wood engravings in the text. *"Ask Mamma"* (London, 1858) was acquired as late as 1947 and includes a set of thirteen plates in hand-colored proofs before letters, eight of which have the legend supplied in Leech's hand-writing and three of which bear his very interesting instructions to the plate printer.

Though collecting books on horses was Clark's initial foray into the bibliophile's world, he did not stop there. By 1916, when he had already begun to build his collection, he wrote to a friend that "horse books keep coming in all the time and so do many others on various subjects. It is a far cry from horse books to Tallement de Reaux . . . Poggio, etc., but it is an actual fact that my searching after books on that glorious animal have led me to find and read a lot of other truck." Hence, Clark began to build a collection of literature which, like that of the books on horses, is composed of major classics in rare editions, with particular emphasis on fine illustrations.

Because no clear pattern emerges as to the development over time of Clark's interests, literary or visual, it can be assumed that Clark's comments to Quaritch Wales in 1939, recorded in his diary, represent his principles from the start. "I was a peculiar collector," writes Clark, "not interested in old books . . . because they were old and rare, [or] Latin texts because of typography, but mostly in texts and illustrated books for fineness of engraving or for costumes and some sporting books. Besides, if I did not like the text I simply did not buy the book!!!"

In fact, Clark did buy a number of "old and rare [and] Latin" books, but it is easy to understand their appeal for a collector interested in illustration. And while there is evidence of at least one purchase of a fifteenth-century illuminated manuscript, Petrarch's *I trionfi*, from the Huth library, with six full-page minia-tures by an artist of the Florentine school, it was with printed books from the late incunabula period onwards that Clark's collection was formed.

The German Renaissance in Nuremberg is finely represented in Hartmann Schedel's *Liber chronicarum* (Nuremberg, 1493), with nearly two thousand wood-cut illustrations by Michael Wolgemut and Wilhelm Pleydenwurff (cat. no. 1). Better known as the Nuremberg Chronicle, this popular world history is the most famous book produced by Anton Koberger. From this same period Clark also acquired superb examples from the Venetian press of Aldus Manutius. An unusual addition was a rare Aldine Virgil of 1514, unillustrated, but printed on blue paper with illuminated initials and in a Grolier binding. Clark obtained several other unillustrated but well-printed and beautifully bound books from the Rahir sale that bear French royal and noble armorials.

The Aldine press was responsible for one of the finest books of all time, Colonna's *Hypnerotomachia Poliphili* (Venice, 1499), which also numbered among Clark's acquisitions. Its 170 woodcuts by an unknown artist were largely responsible for the book's commercial success. In addition, Clark also added to his collection the sixteenth-century French translation of this work (cat. no. 4). Printed in 1546 by the Parisian Jacques Kerver, its variously attributed illustrations were adapted from those in the Aldine edition.

The majority of additions to his library from this period through the eighteenth century were French, a language in which, he wrote, "there seems to be a more varied lot of literature." This same letter of 1916 notes that he is "deep in the *Heptameron*" by Marguerite d'Angoulême, which he would possess in many editions, the most notable, acquired in 1917, being that of 1547 from the famous Lyons partnership of Jacques de Tournes and Bernard Salomon. Salomon's illustrations, appearing in the second volume, are typically small-scale and de Tournes's elegant ornaments and decorated initials are evident throughout.

Clark felt that Montaigne's *Journal du voyage en Italie* was "a perfect treat," and he owned a copy of the first edition, published in 1774, 182 years after the author's death. He also owned four editions of Montaigne's *Essais*, his copy of the 1595 edition bearing the bookplate of Edouard Rahir and bound in an elaborate contemporary gilt *molle*, or flexible, binding incorporating the repeated monogram of Maximilien de Béthune, Duc de Sully. Clark also wrote of "tackling" Rabelais, which he collected in various editions, including a rare two-volume set of *Les oeuvres* published in 1580 by Pierre Estiard in Lyons. Bearing the bookplates of J. P. Chevalier de Saint-Amand, L. A. Barbet, and Cortlandt F. Bishop, this copy is preserved in early seventeenth-century bindings attributed to Florimund Badier and executed for the French chancellor Pierre Séguier (1588-1672) with his initials impressed on the spines.

Clark's literature of the seventeenth century similarly consists of the great French classics—Corneille, Molière, and Racine. While these works were rarely illustrated in first edition, they frequently contain examples of the engraved frontispiece, made popular in the Baroque period. Represented in Clark's collection are many examples of this art by some of the most important artists of the period. For example, the first edition of Pierre Corneille's *La mort de Pompée* (Paris, 1644) contains a classically figured frontispiece by François Chauveau (cat. no. 8). Among the many editions of Molière is the first edition of his *Oeuvres* (Paris, 1666), the frontispiece in each of the two volumes displaying a fanciful illustration, also by Chauveau. And the first edition of Jean Baptiste Racine's *Phèdre et Hippolyte* (Paris, 1677) contains a frontispiece engraved by Sebastien Le Clerc after the design of Charles Le Brun, then court painter.

Illustrated editions from the seventeenth century in Clark's collection include Corneille's *Andromède* (Rouen, 1651), with six engraved plates by Chauveau after Giacomo Torelli's set designs which are splendid examples of the

Baroque imagination (cat. no. 10). Clark also found the first illustrated edition of Molière's *Oeuvres* (Paris, 1682), eight volumes containing thirty-four plates by Pierre Brissart.

The seventeenth-century courtly festival book is represented by *Le jardin de la noblesse françoise* . . . (Paris, 1629), the plates by Abraham Bosse celebrating the manner of costume of the aristocracy during the reign of Louis XIII. This is one of the earliest imprints of costume books in Clark's collection, another being an unusual collection of plates by Nicolas, Henri, Robert, and Jean Baptiste Bonnart, executed circa 1690-1707 and illustrating the costume of the reign of Louis XIV.

The age of the Rococo in France was a very prolific era for book illustrators, and Clark purchased several superb examples of their work, characterized by the use of engraved vignettes, headpieces, tailpieces, and plates on an intimate scale. While the full flowering of this art did not appear until the latter half of the eighteenth century, there is one item of note in Clark's collection which is representative of the transitional years.

In 1939 Clark first mentions his quest for the "Regent's book," Longus's *Les amours pastorales de Daphnis et Chloé*, illustrated by Philippe d'Orléans (Paris, 1718). Rejecting a copy bound by Derome le jeune offered by Drake, Clark wanted to "wait for an extra fine copy in an extra fine binding." In 1940 he found just that and spent a few frantic days finalizing the purchase from the firm of A. S. W. Rosenbach. This copy was assembled from sheets once belonging to the Regent's valet (cat. no. 14). It was bound in London by Charles Kalthoeber and includes a handwritten copy of the Regent's list of subjects which he intended to design, only a part of which were actually executed. Clark also found a copy of the 1724 edition of this work in unfolded sheets and loose plates.

Because so many worthy productions from Clark's collection appeared in the second half of the eighteenth century, it is desirable to give primary attention to the illustrators responsible for the creation of the "four masterpieces of book illustration" of this era as described by Owen E. Holloway.[5] His list includes Boccaccio's *Décaméron* (Paris, 1757-1761), with illustrations by Gravelot; La Fontaine's *Contes et nouvelles* (Paris, 1762), with illustrations by Eisen; La Borde's *Choix de chansons* (Paris, 1773), with illustrations by Moreau le jeune; and Dorat's *Fables nouvelles* (The Hague and Paris, 1773), with illustrations by Marillier. Of these, Clark probably owned only the second and third, but each of these artists is well represented in his collection.

Perhaps Clark first came to know the work of Hubert François Bourguignon, called Gravelot, as an illustrator for the French translation of Fielding's *Tom Jones* (Paris, 1750). It is known that he bought the first English edition of the novel

(London, 1749) as early as 1922. In any case, Clark surely admired Gravelot's illustrations, for he eventually acquired two copies of the French edition—one bearing the bookplate of Edouard Rahir, the other bearing the bookplates of Edouard Moura and Léon Rattier. But while Clark did not own the *Décaméron* of 1757-1761,[6] he did find the *deluxe* edition of Marmontel's *Contes moraux* (Paris, 1765), for which Gravelot provided twenty-four illustrations of equal accomplishment.

Erasmus's *L'éloge de la folie* (Paris, 1751) was the earliest notable success in Charles Eisen's career as an illustrator, and Clark's copy is only the first of many more of Eisen's artistic successes found in his library. Of particular note is the previously mentioned 1762, or *Fermiers-Généraux*, edition of La Fontaine's *Contes et nouvelles*, in which Eisen's designs for the eighty plates are complemented by Pierre Philippe Choffard's fifty-three tailpieces and four vignettes. Clark found two copies of this edition, one of which is in a contemporary binding by Derome le jeune (cat. no. 19).

The illustrations of Jean Michel Moreau, called Moreau le jeune, also appealed to Clark's eye, and at an early stage in his pursuit. Clark's first purchase, in 1917, was the 1773 edition of Molière's *Oeuvres*, containing thirty-three plates designed by Moreau. In total, Clark added fifteen titles with Moreau's illustrations in addition to his "masterpiece," La Borde's *Choix de chansons*, in a copy containing three pages of verse said to be in the handwriting of La Borde (cat. no. 21). Clark's most cherished eighteenth-century acquisition, purchased in 1930, was the *Suite d'estampes pour servir à l'histoire des moeurs et du costume des françois dans le dix-huitième siècle*, which contains thirty-six plates after Moreau and Sigmund Freudeberg (cat. no. 22). Better known as *Monument du costume*, the title under which a portion of it was republished in 1789, this was also a very early purchase. As early as 1923 he looked at various original drawings for this work by Moreau le jeune, eventually acquiring *Cephis with Dog*, a study for plate no. 21 entitled *Le rendez-vous pour Marly*.

Of the four illustrators given prominence by Holloway, Clément Pierre Marillier is the least represented in Clark's collection, which includes only three examples of his work. The best, acquired in 1916, is the third edition of Louvet de Couvray's *Les amours de Chevalier de Faublas* (Paris, 1798), with twenty-seven erotic illustrations by Marillier and others which freely depict scenes from this licentious novel.

One of the great collaborative productions of French Rococo book illustration is Ovid's *Métamorphoses* (Paris, 1767-1771), which brought together the work of Boucher, Gravelot, Eisen, Choffard, Moreau le jeune, and Monnet (cat. no. 20). Clark owned two copies of this work, one of which was supplemented with 175 early states of the plates. This copy, no longer in the collection, was bound by Thibaron-Joly and bears the bookplate of Pierre van Loo.[7]

Clark also owned a number of lavish editions published by Pierre Didot in the 1790s and into the next century. Didot's most famous productions were his Neoclassical *Louvre éditions*, illustrated by artists from the school of David. But Clark apparently was not interested in these. Instead, he bought an edition of La Fontaine's *Contes et nouvelles* (Paris, 1795), illustrated by Fragonard, in a copy containing seventy-one early proofs of the plates,[8] and two works illustrated with imaginative designs by Pierre Paul Prud'hon: Bernard's *Oeuvres* (Paris, 1797) in a copy containing each of the four plates in two states (cat. no. 25) and Longus's *Daphnis et Chloé* (Paris, 1800).

The illustrated book in nineteenth-century France progressed through a variety of artistic media and styles, most of which are represented in Clark's collection. From the early part of the century are examples of the work of Georges Jacques Gatine, the leading costume engraver of the era, including Horace Vernet's *Incroyables et merveilleuses* (Paris, 1814), an album of hand-colored plates engraved by Gatine after Vernet's designs, acquired at the Bishop sale of 1938. The collection also yields examples from the age of Romanticism, when lithography was explored and relief printing was revived. In addition, there are many fine examples of the satirical sentiment expressed in caricature and numerous books from the years of the Belle Epoque, of which Clark was particularly fond.

The most famous examples of early Romantic lithography, illustrations by artists such as Théodore Géricault and Eugène Delacroix are conspicuously absent.[9] But Clark did obtain a copy of *Les contes du gay sçavoir* (Paris, 1828) by J. A. F. Langlé, a book of fables imitative of Parisian printed books of hours of the late fifteenth century, with seven hand-colored lithographs by the Englishman Richard Parkes Bonington and four by the caricaturist Henry Monnier (cat. no. 29).

Honoré Daumier was the master of the art of caricature, rivaled perhaps only by Guillaume Sulpice Chevallier, known as Paul Gavarni. It is interesting that Clark owned only two albums of Daumier's lithographs, but collected seven of Gavarni's. The best of these are *Les lorettes* (Paris, 1841-1843), of which Clark found two complete copies of the seventy-nine lithographs, one in which the plates are hand colored (cat. no. 32), and *Masques et visages* (Paris, 1852-1853), a collection of 329 lithographs. Gavarni was also one of the many artists at this time who designed illustrations to be engraved on wood. While Gavarni's engraved work is not represented, Clark did collect works by other masters of this medium, including Tony Johannot and Auguste Raffet.

Tony Johannot was known for his title vignettes, wonderfully represented in Clark's collection by those for Victor Hugo's *Notre Dame de Paris* (Paris, 1831). Johannot's illustrations are also among the ninety-five plates after various artists, engraved on copper, for Béranger's *Chansons* (Paris, 1829-1833), five volumes of poetry in the Napoleonic tradition. Another contributor to this work was Auguste Raffet, whose illustrations for Fieffé's *Napoléon Ier et la garde impériale* (Paris, 1859) also celebrate the Napoleonic legend which emerges as an important theme in Clark's collection.

Gustave Doré and Edouard Manet were responsible for the most successful illustrations in the third quarter of the nineteenth century. Clark's collection yields examples only of Doré's work, the most important being *Les contes drolatiques* (Paris, 1855) by Honoré de Balzac, with 425 wood-engraved vignettes, head- and tailpieces (cat. no. 35), illustrations representative of Doré's typically haunting style. But his lighter mood, expressed in the medium of lithography, is also represented in two albums, *Les différents publics de Paris* (Paris, 1854) and *La ménagerie parisienne* of the same year.

Clark's instructions to James Drake in 1929 were "to look after books of 1880 to 1900 which had texts & were illustrated at the time." Although he often found the "reproduction processes for illustration extremely crude," Clark acquired numerous examples from the Belle Epoque. However, not all of the volumes in his collection from this period "had texts"; for example, the albums of lithographs by Jean Louis Forain and Caran d'Ache. But the many works of literature with illustrations by Madeleine Lemaire and Henriot must have been just what he had in mind.

Madeleine Lemaire, who was primarily a flower painter, was a member of the Société Nationale des Beaux-Arts. Examples of her illustrations in Clark's collection include Ludovic Halévy's *L'Abbé Constantin* (Paris, 1888) and Paul Hervieu's *Flirt* (Paris, 1890), both of which were contemporary best sellers. Clark owned two copies of the latter, one of which was a presentation copy to the illustrator from the publisher, Boussod Valadon et Cie. It was bound by Durvand, with the monogram ML on the front cover. The other copy, one of twenty printed on Whatman paper, contains an original signed watercolor and was bound by Zaehnsdorf. Lemaire's work for both of these novels clearly reveals her association with the academy.

Henri Maigrot, called Henriot, is known best for his humorous contributions to the journals *Charivari* and *Illustration*. Clark found five examples of his illustrated books, including *La famille Cardinal* (Paris, 1883) by Ludovic Halévy, the illustrations for which are original watercolors placed in the margins (cat. no. 38). Of the numbered edition of fifty, Clark's copy is number thirty-six and once belonged to Robert Hoe. Robert Hoe also once owned, and Cortlandt F. Bishop after him, Clark's copy of Octave Feuillet's *Julia de Trécourt* (Paris, 1885), which contains Henriot's original drawings for the fifteen engraved illustrations. In addition, it includes a watercolor on the half-title page and two additional sets of the plates in various states.

Clark's interests in nineteenth-century book illustration also extended to artists working in England, where styles developed similarly to those in France. English examples of the art of caricature in Clark's collection are found in the work of Thomas Rowlandson and George Cruikshank, who, like Gavarni in France, depicted scenes of everyday life. In addition, the collection offers many more examples of the work of John Leech, whose sporting illustrations have already been discussed. Leech is equally known for his illustrations for the novels of Charles Dickens. It is interesting to note that when, in 1926, Clark first considered *A Christmas Carol*, which contains Leech's best work, he "cursed out Dickens." But convinced by Drake that it "was fine," he bought, in 1932, all five of Dickens's Christmas books.

The middle of the century is also represented by the work of William Makepeace Thackeray, Richard Doyle, and Sir John Tenniel. It is difficult to determine whether Clark's interest in the works of Thackeray was sparked by his appreciation of Thackeray's illustrations or his writings. In any case, Clark's interest certainly went beyond the fad that Thackeray's works enjoyed among pre-Depression American collectors. In 1923 Clark bought the extremely rare, unillustrated first edition of *The Second Funeral of Napoleon* (London, 1841) and in 1927 purchased from Drake six Christmas books which were published between 1847 and 1855, five of which were illustrated by the author. In 1927, Drake also supplied Thackeray's first published book, *Flore et Zephyr* (London, 1836), a rare album of colored lithographs satirizing the ballet. Thackeray's illustrations also appear in three of his major works, *Vanity Fair* (London, 1847-1848, cat. no. 34), *The History of Pendennis* (London, 1848-1850), and *The Virginians* (London, 1857-1859), all of which Clark aquired in the original, serially issued parts. As late as 1948, Clark acquired a collection of original autograph manuscripts, letters, drawings, and sketches which had been formed by Thackeray's granddaughter.

The only examples of Richard Doyle's masterful illustrations that Clark collected are those which were provided for texts by Thackeray. This suggests that Clark was not interested in Doyle's work, per se, especially since one of these, *Rebecca and Rowena* (London, 1850), Thackeray's Christmas book which appeared in 1850, was bought together with the five other Christmas books mentioned above. Thackeray's *The Newcomes* (London, 1853-1855) in original monthly parts is the other book illustrated by Doyle in Clark's collection.

When in 1926 Clark first bought Lewis Carroll's *Alice's Adventures in Wonderland*, with forty-two illustrations by Sir John Tenniel, he returned it in a few months' time, claiming "it is rot." While it is not known which edition he had in his hand at that time, it must be assumed that at some point Clark changed his mind about Carroll, or developed an interest in the illustrator, Sir John Tenniel, for his collection does include a copy of the first American edition (New York, 1866) of this work.

The end of the century in England is represented by a group of artists whose common appeal for Clark was their illustrations for the writings of Rudyard Kipling. The *Series of Thirty Etchings by William Strang Illustrating the Subjects from the Writings of Rudyard Kipling* (London, 1901) is the most important illustrated Kipling work in Clark's collection. Others include William Nicholson's *An Almanac of Twelve Sports* (London, 1898), an album of twelve hand-colored woodcuts accompanying verses by Kipling; *'They'* (London, 1905), with illustrations by F. H. Townsend; and *Sea and Sussex* (London, 1926), illustrated by Donald Maxwell. Clark bought as many as three copies of the latter in addition to a watercolor drawing for it entitled *North Sea Patrol*.

Clark bought these four books to enhance his Kipling collection. He started to acquire Kipling's work in 1922 with the purchase of *Plain Tales From the Hills* (Calcutta, 1888), of which he would eventually own four copies, including an autographed presentation copy of the first issue. Clark continued to add Kipling material through 1950, his last purchase being an autographed manuscript of the unpublished poem "A Ballad of Bitterness," dedicated to Kipling's mother and signed "Boy." All together, Clark accumulated some 225 items, buying both newly published works such as *The Fox Meditates* (London, 1933) and excessively rare works such as *Departmental Ditties* (Lahore, 1886), presented to "the Common Room, U.S. [United Services] College," and containing manuscript notes by the author explaining the Indian words and phrases contained in the poems.

If Clark ever doubted his continued investment in Kipling material, it was in 1936 when he questioned Drake about the writer's popularity. He was quick to agree, however, and "never heard Kipling better described," when Marston Drake replied, "Kipling is the only author whose varied works have a universal appeal. Many people do not like this or that but there are always some things of his they do like."

Clark spent a good deal of time at the Drake establishment discussing the book trade and the quality of his investments. When an important sale approached, Clark would consult them regarding his bids. But Clark himself did not attend the sales and even cautioned friends against it, preferring to remain anonymous. It is also true that Francine Clark never accompanied her husband to the book dealers, where conversation, as recorded in his diaries, soon drifted to the realm of international politics and the economic crises of the '30s. But while Clark very much valued the advice given by the Drakes, he did not always heed it. When Clark took home, on their advice, Thornton Wilder's *The Bridge of San Luis Rey*, he returned it almost immediately, saying "it is like cubist art," noting, however, that its value had risen twenty percent in the meantime.

Like the other collections (which do not include examples of cubism) Clark's collection of books displays the tastes of an individual. That Clark was fond of saying "I am not an archaeologist, but a collector" is indicative of his tendency to acquire only that which he admired and not to attempt to form a representative or historical survey of great works. Clark's tastes, so far as the book collection reveals, included an admiration for horse books, acquired initially for his edification, but eventually for the illustrations contained within. He also enjoyed costume books and literature, primarily in the French language, which he acquired in numerous, rare editions, often finely illustrated. His literary tastes also included English literature and exhibit a particular fondness for Kipling.

The Library of the Sterling and Francine Clark Art Institute has acquired, through gift and purchase, other illustrated books of high artistic merit which complement Clark's collection. Several have been included in this exhibition. However, the forty-two books exhibited and described on the following pages, in large measure, display the individual tastes of Robert Sterling Clark.

Susan Roeper

1. Hans P. Kraus, *A Rare Book Saga: the Autobiography of H. P. Kraus* (New York: G. P. Putnam's Sons, 1978), 301.
2. Ibid., 299.
3. As cited by John B. Podeschi, comp., *Books on the Horse and Horsemanship: Riding, Hunting, Breeding & Racing, 1400-1941*, Sport in Art and Books: The Paul Mellon Collection (London: The Tate Gallery for the Yale Center for British Art, 1981), cat. no. 64.
4. Gordon N. Ray, *The Illustrator and the Book in England from 1790 to 1914* (New York: The Pierpont Morgan Library, 1976), 32, 84.
5. Owen E. Holloway, *French Rococo Book Illustration* (London: A. Trianti, 1969), 1.
6. The Library of the Sterling and Francine Clark Art Institute added this work to the collection in 1985 (see cat. no. 17).
7. This copy is described in Gordon N. Ray, *The Art of the French Illustrated Book 1700-1914* (New York: The Pierpont Morgan Library, 1982), cat. no. 62B.
8. This copy, no longer in the collection, is also described in ibid., cat. no. 77.
9. The Library acquired, in 1989, Goethe's *Faust* (1828) illustrated by Delacroix (see cat. no. 28).

CATALOGUE OF
THE EXHIBITION

NOTES TO THE CATALOGUE

THE BOOKS ARE LISTED CHRONOLOGICALLY by date of publication. The author, title, place of publication, publisher, and publication date are given. Five additional items are then detailed: (a) the sequence of printed pages expressed in leaves (*l.*) or pages (*p.*) and leaves of plates; (b) the height and width of the page (the largest is measured if there is variation) in inches and millimeters; (c) a brief description of the binding: ¼ is with leather back or spine only; ½ is with leather corners which, measured with the spine leather, cover less than ½ of the top edge of the board; ¾ is with larger leather corners; (d) evidence in the book of previous ownership; (e) the source or means by which the book entered the Library of the Sterling and Francine Clark Art Institute. For definitions of standard terms and abbreviations used in the description of books and their decoration, see John Carter, *A B C for Book Collectors* (New York: Alfred A. Knopf, 1987).

REFERENCES

BERALDI   Beraldi, Henri. *Les graveurs du XIXe siècle.* 12 vols. Paris: L. Conquet, 1885-1892.

BMC   *Catalogue of Books Printed in the XVth Century now in the British Museum.* 11 parts. London: British Museum, 1908-1985.

BRIVOIS   Brivois, Jules. *Bibliographie des ouvrages illustrés du XIXe siècle.* 1883. Reprint. Hildesheim and New York: G. Olms, 1974.

BRUN   Brun, Robert. *Le livre français illustré de la Renaissance.* Paris: A. et J. Picard, 1969.

BRUNET   Brunet, Jacques Charles. *Manuel du libraire et de l'amateur de livres. . . .* 5th ed. 1860. Reprint. 8 vols. in 7. Paris: G.-P. Maisonneuve & Larose, 1965-1966.

CARTERET   Carteret, Léopold. *Le trésor du bibliophile romantique et moderne, 1801-1875.* Paris: L. Carteret, 1927.

CARTERET 1946   Carteret, Léopold. *Le trésor du bibliophile: livres illustrés modernes, 1875 á 1945. . . .* 5 vols. Paris: L. Carteret, 1946-1948.

COHEN-DE RICCI   Cohen, Henry. *Guide de l'amateur de livres á gravures de XVIIIe siècle.* Revised and enlarged by Seymour de Ricci. 6th ed. 2 vols. in 1. Paris: A Rouquette, 1912.

FOWLER   Fowler, Laurence Hall, and Elizabeth Baer. *The Fowler Architectural Collection of the Johns Hopkins University: Catalogue.* 1961. Reprint. Woodbridge, Conn.: Research Publications, 1982.

FRIEDMAN   Friedman, Joan M. *Color Printing in England, 1486-1870.* Exhibition catalogue. New Haven: Yale Center for British Art, 1978.

GOFF   Goff, Frederick Richmond. *Incunabula in American Libraries. . . .* New York: Bibliographical Society of America, 1964.

MELLON   Podeschi, John B., comp. *Books on the Horse and Horsemanship: Riding, Hunting, Breeding & Racing, 1400-1941.* Sport in Art and Books: The Paul Mellon Collection. London: The Tate Gallery for the Yale Center for British Art, 1981.

MORTIMER   Mortimer, Ruth. *Harvard College Library, Department of Printing and Graphic Arts . . . French Sixteenth Century Books.* 2 vols. Cambridge, Mass.: Harvard University Press, 1964.

MURRAY   Davies, Hugh W. *Catalogue of a Collection of Early French Books in the Library of C. Fairfax Murray.* 2 vols. London: Privately printed, 1910.

MURRAY 1913   Davies, Hugh W. *Catalogue of a Collection of Early German Books in the Library of C. Fairfax Murray*. 2 vols. London: Privately printed, 1913.

RAHIR   *La bibliothèque de feu Edouard Rahir*. Auction catalogues. 6 vols. Paris: F. Lefrançois, 1930-1938.

RAY   Ray, Gordon N. *The Art of the French Illustrated Book, 1700-1914*. New York: The Pierpont Morgan Library, 1982.

RAY 1976   Ray, Gordon N. *The Illustrator and the Book in England from 1790-1914*. New York: The Pierpont Morgan Library, 1976.

ROSCOE   Roscoe, S. *Thomas Bewick: a Bibliography Raisonné. . . .* 1953. Reprint. Folkestone and London: Dawsons of Pall Mall, 1973.

ROSENWALD   United States Library of Congress. *The Lessing J. Rosenwald Collection. . . .* Washington: Library of Congress, 1977.

SKIRA   Skira, Albert. *Anthologie du livre illustré par le peintres et sculpteurs de l'école de Paris. . . .* Geneva: A. Skira, 1946.

VAN DUZER   Van Duzer, Henry Sayre. *A Thackeray Library: First Editions and Publications . . . Collected by Henry Sayre Van Duzer*. New York: Privately printed, 1919.

VICAIRE   Vicaire, Georges. *Manuel de l'amateur de livres du XIXe siècle. . . .* 8 vols. Paris: A. Rouquette, 1894-1920.

1. HARTMANN SCHEDEL

Liber chronicarum. Nuremberg, Anton Koberger, 12 July 1493. [20], 266, [6], 267-299, [1] *l. There are three numbered blank leaves: 259, 260, 261.* All leaves are mounted on stubs.[1] Page size: 17¼ x 11½ in. (439 x 286 mm.) Binding: 17th-century vellum. Round embossed bookplate with monogram of Ricardo Heredia. Robert Sterling Clark Collection.

ILLUSTRATIONS: Woodcut title page;[2] 645 different woodcuts, of which 1,164 are repeated one or more times, for a total of 1,809 illustrations by Michael Wolgemut and Wilhelm Pleydenwurff; calligraphic pen initials in reddish-brown ink, colored in red and blue; red and blue rubrication throughout the book.

REFERENCES: BMC II, 437; Brunet I, 1860; Goff S-307; Murray 1913, 394.[3]

NOTES:

1. The leaves have been trimmed at the inner margin and mounted on stubs, apparently because of severe water damage along the gutter. As a result, small portions of the illustrations are lost along the inner edges.

2. The calligraphic woodcut title page is the title for the index. It reads as follows: Registrum huius operis libri cronicarum cu[m] figuris et ymagi[ni]bus ab inicio mu[n]di.

3. The Clark copy collates exactly as the British Museum copy, with all leaves bound in the same order.

4. The documentation is reproduced, translated, and discussed in Adrian Wilson, assisted by Joyce Lancaster Wilson, *The Making of the Nuremberg Chronicle* (Amsterdam: Nico Israel, 1976). A German edition followed the Latin one. Probably fifteen hundred Latin and one thousand German copies were printed.

The *Liber chronicarum*, better known as the Nuremberg Chronicle, is one of the great books of the fifteenth century. Monumental in size and masterfully executed, it is also one of the few incunabula (books printed before 1501) for which sufficient documentation survives in the form of manuscript layout pages and contracts to allow us to follow much of its creation.[4]

From information supplied in the colophons, we know the names of the principals involved in the work. The text was composed by Hartmann Schedel (1440-1514), a physician from Nuremberg; the underwriters of the project were Sebald Schreyer, a wealthy Nuremberg merchant, and his brother-in-law Sebastian Kammermaister. The printer Anton Koberger (1440-1513) was among the most renowned and prolific in Germany, carrying on a trade in books all over Europe. The artists providing the illustrations were Michael Wolgemut (1434-1519) and Wilhelm Pleydenwurff (d. 1494). Wolgemut had a large workshop which produced altarpieces, sculpture, playing cards, and paintings as well as prints.

The text of the Chronicle follows the pattern of previous Christian world chronicles. It is in no way original but is borrowed freely from earlier sources, even when it deals with contemporary events.

The illustrations are carefully integrated with the text and take up almost as much space; it is a rare page that has no illustrations at all. The figures in the genealogical tables are connected by sinewy branches that run in and around the text. Most of the figures do multiple service, so that the same crowned, mitred, or haloed bust is used for different kings, bishops, or saints. The same is true of several city views, as well.

Stylistically the cuts are typical of the late fifteenth century in their angularity, their sharply delineated, multiple drapery folds, and their use of decorative elements derived from flamboyant late Gothic architecture. Yet many cuts are expressive, such as the "Dance of Death," and pictorial in the extensive use of cross-hatched modeling, in the use of cast shadows and reflections in the water, in the attempt to render texture of materials, and in the occasional suggestion of aerial perspective.

The illustration shows a view of Jerusalem, a purely graphic scene with no hint of pictorial devices such as aerial perspective. Nevertheless, it is of interest in its portrayal of the Temple of Solomon, neatly labeled, at the center of the city. We also see clearly an effort to depict portions of the walls and doors that are in shadow.

S.S.G.

Ierosolima nomē vrbis in palestina me
tropolis iudeoz:prī Ieb°. postea salē.
Stercio hierosolima. vltio belia dicta. Cu
ius vrbis prim° odditor fuit (vt Joseph° testat)
Canaan q iust° appellat° erat rex. Et b q̃ē mel
chisedech sacerdos dei altissimi dicebatur. Qui
cu ibidē phanū edificasss illud Solima appella
uit. solimi fuerūt ppli iuxta liciā q̃s homer° pul
gnatissimos: z a bellerophōte deuictos dicit. et
in mōtib° hitasse. Et corneli° tacit° cū de iudeoz
origine opionē narrat ait. Illi clara iudeoz ini
tia solimos carmib° celebratā homeri gētē odi
tam vrbē hierosolimā noie suo fecisse. vn Juue
nalis interpres legū solimaz. q̃ ciuitas cananee
gētis vsq̃ ad tpa dauid regi hitatio fuit. Nec io
sue iudeoz priceps eos cananeos seu iebuseos
expellere potuit. Dauid iebuseis expulsis cū ci
uitatem reedificasset eā hierosolimā. i. munitissi
mā nūcupauit. Huj° vrb situs z munitio petro
sa erat. z triplici muro cingebatur. q̃ vt Strabo
ait inter° ade abundans exter° vo oino siccam
fossam hēbat i lapide excisam. xl. pedū pfundi
tate. latitudo vo. cc. l. E lapide aūt exciso educta
erant celeberrimi tēpli menia. Hec hierosolima
lōge clarissima vrbium oziētis sup̃ duos colles
erat odita iteruallo discretos i quā vom° creber
rime desinebāt. Colliū alter q̃ superor citas excel
sior z i plurixate directior castellū dauid dicebat
tur. Alter q̃ iserioze° sustinet citates vndiq̃ declu
uis° e vall i medio ad syloā ptinj ita fōte q̃ dulc̃
e vocabāt. firmissime āt dō salomōis alioruq̃ i

terra regū opa oznata fuit. agrippa eē ptez citat̃
addiderat z cinxerat. Exuberās eīn mlltitudine
paulati extra menia bpebat. Noiata e ps addi
ta noua citas. Oīe āt citat̃ i giro spaciū. xxx. z
trib° stadijs finiebat. Et si i toto admirabil. ter
cius mur° admirabilior ob excellētias turr̃ q̃ ad
septētrione occidētēq̃ surgeb at i agulo. de q̃ so
le otto arabia pspici poterat z mare vsq̃ ad fi
nes hebreoz. Et iuxta eā turr̃ yppico: z due q̃s
herodes i ātiq̃ muro edificauerat. Mirabil fuit
lapidū magnitudo ex secto marmoze cādido ita
aduati vt single turres singla sarauideree .hijs
i septētriōali pte aula cū pstātissima ziugeba
tur. Muro alto cincta ac varietate saxoz oznata
Ante deniq̃ portie p circlm flexe columec i sin
gulis:q̃ iter eas sb diuo patebāt spacia vbi erāt
viridaria cū cisternis eneis. qb°aq̃ effundebat.
Pudet dicere b regia q̃ fuerat cū flāma ab iestī
nis isidiatorib° oīa psumpsit. De excidio tū h°
regie vrb itern° patebit; vrbē aūt sacraz reddidit
mors xpi. Placz sac i eo loco videre possumus
Amne. s. q̃ lot° e xps. Tēplū seu tēpli ruinaz i q̃
vcouit. locū vbi cū sūma hūilitate passus e corpe
vt nos aī passionib° libaret. sepulcz vbi sactissi
mū illd corp° pstitit. Et vn ascedit in celū. q̃ ad
iudiciū reuersur° credit. vbi vet̃ z fluctib° ipauit
vbi deiq̃ elegit idoctos atz iopes piscatores. q̃
rū bamis z rhetib° piscaret ipatores z reges gē
tius. vbi cecos illluauit. leprosos mūdauit. pa
raliticos erexit. mortuos suscitauit. Multaq̃z
alia q̃ lōge pseq̃ tediosū cet. cū ex euāge. nō sint

¶ Porta ccrglan̄   ¶ HIEROSOLIMA   ¶ Porta vall' iosaphat

Porta vet° siue
iudiciala

Porta piloatie pisciue

TEPLVM·SALOMOIS·

Porta pilou
ul'daud

Porta auti
vial

2. JEAN MILLES DE SOUVIGNY

Praxis criminis persequendi,
elegantibus aliquot figuris illustrata
Joanne Millaeo Bo[io] Sylvigniaco.
Paris: apud Simonem Colinaeum,
1541. [4], 85 *l. There are five errors in
numbering: 22 numbered 23; 43 numbered
46; 45 not numbered; 54 numbered 51;
62 numbered 16.* Page size:
12¹⁵⁄₁₆ x 8¼ in. (312 x 210 mm.)
Binding: Full red morocco gilt by
Chambolle-Duru. Robert Sterling
Clark Collection.

ILLUSTRATIONS: Woodcut title-page
cartouche, woodcut coat of arms verso
of title page, 13 full-page woodcuts,
and 3 sizes of *criblé* initials (2 large,
8 medium, 13 small) attributed to
Geoffroy de Tory.

REFERENCES: Brun 250; Brunet III,
1715; Rahir 1492.

NOTES:

1. Mortimer 374 and Rahir 599 describe
   the issue with the L'Angelier brothers'
   names on the title page.

2. Brun sees Jollat's hand in the *Praxis*
   woodcuts because of the resemblance
   to a style related to Basel; Jollat evi-
   dently had Basel connections through
   the printer Chrestien Wechel, who
   also printed in Paris from 1522 to
   1526. Certainly the prints appear to
   be within a German rather than a
   French tradition.

3. A list of subjects is given in Philippe
   Rénouard, *Bibliographie des éditions de
   Simon de Colines, 1520-1546* (Paris:
   Paul, Huard et Guillemin, 1984),
   342-343, 468.

The *Praxis criminis* by Jean Milles de Souvigny (d. 1563) was published in 1541 by the distinguished French printer Simon de Colines (1475-1547). The first edition bears the L'Angelier brothers' names as well as that of Colines on the title page. The Clark copy is another issue of the same year bearing only the name of Colines.[1] Colines was a productive printer publishing some seven hundred works and was largely responsible for the change in French fashion from the older black letter type to roman and italic.

Milles's text gives extensive details of criminal procedure by present- ing imaginary murder scenes, the subsequent interrogation of witnesses, arrest of suspects, torture, trial, and condemnation leading to final execu- tion. The text, ornamented with *criblé*, or dotted, initials in three sizes, is set in a single column of handsome roman letter within the commentary, which is set in two columns in small roman and italic. It also contains thirteen exceptionally fine woodcuts. Often characterized as late Gothic in style, the cuts might better be described as transitional. Distortions of perspective make them seem old-fashioned for the 1540s, but the costumes are contemporary and the architectural backgrounds sometimes contain typical Renaissance motifs such as putti.

There is no agreement as to the identity of the artist, but those proposed have been the important French bookseller, engraver, and printer Geoffroy de Tory (c. 1480-1533); Jean (sometimes called Mercure) Jollat (act. 1530-1546);[2] Jacquemin Woeiriot (act. 1503-1533), engraver and goldsmith for the Duke of Lorraine; and Oronce Finé (1494-1555), the astronomer and printmaker. Without convincing evidence he must for the moment remain anonymous.

Scholars have stressed the close relationship between the text and the illustrations. The illustration shown depicts the arrest of a suspect and the preliminary interrogation.[3] Three different scenes of the narrative are shown within an elaborate architectural setting. Each scene has its own perspective and there is no common vanishing point as is usual with most Renaissance illustrations. The figures in contemporary dress are animated and well modeled. We are able to follow the events of the story quite clearly as it unfolds even without the aid of the labels in the cartouche and the banderole.

S.S.G.

3. GIOVANNI BOCCACCIO

Le decameron de Mesire Jehan Bocace nouvellement traduict d'Italien en Francoys par maistre Anthoine le Macon. Paris: Etienne Roffet, 1545. [7] *l.*, 254 *l.* Page size: 12⅝ x 8¼ in. (319 x 210 mm.) Ruled in red ink. Binding: 17th-century full brown morocco gilt and red morocco gilt doublures.[1] Early signatures of L. M. Monin [?] on front flyleaf and of Anne de Perrevine on last page; bookplate of Edouard Rahir. Robert Sterling Clark Collection.

ILLUSTRATIONS: 10 relief cuts, *criblé* initials.

REFERENCES: Brun 136; Brunet I, 1006, Suppl. 141; Mortimer 106; Murray 40; Rahir 969.

NOTES:

1. According to Rahir 969, the motifs on the binding are found on volumes bound for the Marquis de La Vieuville.

2. For an extensive list of Delaune's prints, see André Linzeler, *Inventaire du fonds français: Graveurs du seizième siècle*, 2 vols. (Paris: Bibliothèque Nationale, 1932-1938), 1: 218-301. The 1545 Boccaccio prints are not included.

*T*he *Decameron* of Giovanni Boccaccio (1313-1375), although composed in the mid-fourteenth century, retains its appeal after more than six centuries. For a note on the great humanist and his masterpiece, see cat. no. 17. The Clark copy is the first edition of Antoine Le Maçon's translation commissioned by Marguerite d'Angoulême, Queen of Navarre, whose own *Heptameron* is modeled on *The Decameron*. Le Maçon's dedication to the Queen was printed in both roman and italic type but, as in most copies, the duplicate leaf has not been included (in this case the one printed in italic).

The book is set in a bold, clear roman letter within margins drawn in red ink. There are four sizes of handsome *criblé*, or dotted background, initials, a popular early sixteenth-century decoration.

The ten illustrations are all set within a border of strapwork and foliated ornament which is repeated throughout the volume. Freely copied from a Venetian edition of 1542, they have been attributed to Etienne Delaune (1518/1519-1583). Brun states that they were printed from metal relief plates rather than from woodblocks. Although Delaune's earliest engraved work is dated from either 1557 or 1561, Mortimer believes he could have done some earlier prints. The use of metal plates would conform with his other professional activities as a goldsmith and engraver of medals. Delaune also produced a number of independent prints; his total output has been estimated at over four hundred, so that his participation in the illustration of *Le décaméron* is not beyond the realm of possibility.[2] The publisher Etienne Roffet was official bookbinder to François Ier and the ornament of the borders has been related to those made by bookbinders. The prints themselves are clearly related to the School of Fontainebleau in their elongation of figure and emphasis on linearity.

The illustration shown pertains to the first tale of the third day in which Masetto de Lamporecchio pretends to be a deaf mute and secures a job as gardener in a convent. His hopes that all the nuns will want to make love to him are fully realized as the women, even the abbess, all compete for his favors. The story is neatly compressed into two scenes divided by a tree and a fence. On the left side some of the nuns admiringly discover Masetto sleeping in the garden, stretched out in a pose reminiscent of a classical shepherd. On the right side a nun (perhaps the abbess?) tugs him by the arm as she receives him at a portal of one of the convent buildings. The scene is executed in sharp outline with delicate shading.

The book as a whole is an excellent example of the best of Renaissance bookmaking, in which an equilibrium of all the different elements is achieved. In Roffet's *Decameron*, type, ornamented letters, illustrations, and pleasing proportions of the page all blend effortlessly together.

S.S.G.

Maſet de Lamporecchio contre-
FAISANT DV MVET, DEVINT IARDI-
nier d'ung monaſtere de femmes, leſquelles coucherent toutes auecques luy.

Nouuelle premiere.

L ya mes tresbelles dames beaucoup d'hommes & de femmes qui ſont ſi folz qu'ilz croient aſſeurement que tout auſſi toſt qu'on à mis à vne ieune fille le voile ſur la teſte & le bâdeau blãc au frõt, & qu'on luy à chargé le doz d'ung capuchõ noir, quelle ne ſoit plus femme: & ne ſente plus les appetitz femenins, ne plus ne moins que ſi elle pour eſtre faicte nõnain eſtoit deuenue pier-re: & ſi par fortune ilz oyent quelque choſe cõtre ceſte leur creance ilz ſen courrouſſent auſſi fort cõme ſi on auoit cõmis vng treſgrant & enorme peché cõtre nature: ſans penſer toutesfois de deuoir auoir quelque cõ-ſideracion à ſoy meſmes, qui la pleine liberté de pouuoir faire ce qu'ilz veulent ne peult ſaouler: ne conſiderantz auſſi les grandes forces de l'oiſiueté, & dela ſoli-tude. Pareillement il y à encor beaucoup de gens qui croyent aſſeurement que la houe & la beſche, les groſſes viandes & les malayſes oſtent du tout les appetitz ſenſuelz de la chair aux laboureurs des châps, & qu'ilz les rendent groſſiers d'en-tendement & de preuoyance: mais ie veulx bien (puis que la royne me la cõman dé, & ſans ſortir hors de ce quelle à propoſé) vous faire certaines auecques vne pe-tite nouuelleté, combien tous ceulx qui le croyent ainſi, ſont trõpez grandement.
En ceſtuy noſtre pays il y eut, & eſt encores vng monaſtere de femmes fort

I iiij   renommé

4. FRANCESCO COLONNA

Hypnerotomachie, ou Discours du songe de Poliphile deduisant comme amour le combat a l'occasion de Polia. Nouvellement traduict de langage Italien en Francois. Paris: Jacques Kerver, 1546. [6], 157, [1] *l.* Page size: 12¹⁵⁄₁₆ x 7⁵⁄₁₆ in. (329 x 186 mm.) Binding: Full red morocco. Autograph of J[ames] Thornhill on title page. Robert Sterling Clark Collection.

ILLUSTRATIONS: Decorated title page, 43 decorated woodcut initials, and 143 woodcuts.

REFERENCES: Brun 156; Brunet IV, 778-779; Mortimer 146; Rahir 1298.

NOTES:

1. A psychological and interpretative summary of the text, the complexity of which is equaled only by that of the critical commentary which has appeared since its original publication, can be found in Linda Fierz-David's *The Dream of Poliphilo* (New York: Pantheon, 1950).

2. Pierre Du Colombier, *Jean Goujon* (Paris: A. Michel, 1949), 138.

The *Hypnerotomachia*, or Love's Strife in a Dream of Poliphilus, is believed to have been composed originally in 1469 by a Dominican monk, Francesco Colonna (d. 1527). It was first printed thirty-two years later by the great Venetian scholar-printer Aldus Manutius (1450-1515). The story is ostensibly a romance in which the lovers Poliphilus and Polia move through a dreamlike landscape. It has been called a mixture of erotic allegory, pagan ritual, and Christian symbolism, interspersed with erudite classical references and elaborate descriptions of ancient architectural components.[1] Although Aldus's first edition was a commercial failure, it was greatly admired for the illustrative woodcuts which in their linear simplicity and grace have been linked both to Andrea Mantegna (1431-1506) and Giovanni Bellini (1430-1516).

The Clark copy is the first edition of the first French translation by Jean Martin. The text is printed in a clear, bold roman letter, forty-five long lines to a page. The cuts have been attributed to the elder Jean Cousin (c. 1490-1560/1561), Jean Goujon (c. 1510-1568), and others. The Goujon attribution is based upon the book's architectural and sculptural features and on Jean Goujon's association with Jean Martin in preparing an edition of Vitruvius in 1547. On the other hand the Goujon attribution has been rejected on the basis of stylistic comparisons with the same Vitruvius and with the publication *L'entrée de Henri II à Paris* of 1549.[2] At least four distinct styles or hands have been identified in the *Hypnerotomachia*, the most accomplished of which is to be seen in the first four scenes of the dream.

The illustrations, while based on the Italian cuts, have been freely adapted with shaded lines and elongated figures in the French Mannerist style and with the addition of more lavish landscapes and architectural detail. Fourteen subjects, all concerned with buildings and gardens, were added to the French edition.

Another feature of the book is the use of large arabesque initials. The initials *M* and *F* on leaves 18 recto and 21 verso were originally printed from *criblé* blocks, but arabesque initials have been pasted over them in most copies, as in this one. Aldus's simple Venetian title page in the 1501 edition has been replaced by Kerver with an elaborate frame of satyrs, fruits, and putti. Two tortoises, a printer's device used by Kerver, can be seen at the bottom.

The illustration shows the beginning of Poliphilus's dream. He stands at the edge of a wood of feathery palm trees contemplating a prospect of classical ruins. A Corinthian capital and a broken caryatid lie in the immediate foreground while a wolf with jaws parted leaps into the remnants of ancient glory scattered on the ground amid the underbrush. The artist, however, does not capture the sense of terror that the text imparts, preferring to emphasize the contemplative aspect of the dream.

S.S.G.

donné ce tiltre qu'elles signifient victoire, pourautant qu'elles resistent a toute charge & pesant faiz sans qu'on les puisse prosterner. En ce lieu n'y auoit
aucune habitation, toutesfois en cheminant entre ces arbres sur main gau-
che m'apparut vn loup courant la gueule pleine, par la veue duquel les che-
ueux me dresserét en la teste, & voulu crier, mais ie ne me trouuay point de
voix. Aussi tost qu'il m'eut apperceu, il s'en fuyt dedás le boys. quoy voiát ie
retournay aucunemét en moy, & leuát les yeulx deuers celle part ou les mó-
taignes s'assembloient, ie vey vn peu a costiere vne grande haulteur en for-
me d'vne tour, & la aupres vn bastimét qui sembloit imperfaict, toutesfois
a ce que i'en pouoie iuger, c'estoit de structure antique.

Du costé ou estoit cest edifice, les cotaulx se leuoient vn peu plus hault, &
sembloiét ioindre au bastiment qui estoit assis entre deux montaignes, & ser
uoit de closture a vne vallée: parquoy estimant que c'estoit chose digne de
veoir, i'adressay mon chemin celle part. mais tant plus i'en approchoye, plus
se descouuroit ceste œuure magnifique, & me croissoit le desir de la regarder,
car elle ne resembloit plus vne tour, ains vn merueilleux obelisque, fondé
sur vn grand monceau de pierres, la haulteur duquel excedoit sans cóparai-
son les montaignes qui estoient aux deux costez. Quand ie fu approché tout
pres, ie m'arrestai pour contempler plus a loisir si gráde insolence d'architecture qui estoit a demy demolie, cóposee de quartiers de marbre blác assem-
blez sans cyment, & si bien adioustez, que la ou elle estoit encores entiere, la
pointe d'vne aiguille n'eust sceu entrer entre deux pierres. La y auoit de toutes sortes de colonnes, partie tumbées & rompues, partie entieres: & en leurs
lieux, auec leurs chapiteaux, architraués, frizes, cornices, & soubassemens, de
                                                                    A iiij

5. OVID

La vita et metamorfoseo d'Ovidio, figurata & abbreviato in forma d'epigrammi da M. Gabriello Symeoni. Con altre stanze sopra gl'effetti della Luna; il ritratto d'una fontana d'Overnia; & un apologia generale nella fine del libro. Lione: Giovanni di Tornes, 1559. 245, [59] p. Page size: 6⅜ x 4⁹⁄₁₆ in. (157 x 116 mm.) Binding: 17th-century vellum. Ownership inscription, p. 12, of Gio. Pietro Pozzo, 7 giunio, 1662, in Piacenza. Purchase 1988.

ILLUSTRATIONS: Title-page medallion portrait; added bordered title page (p. 157); added title page (p. 269); 189 woodcuts with borders and 7 woodcuts without borders.

REFERENCES: Brun 264; Brunet IV, 287, Suppl. 117; Mortimer 405.

NOTES:

1. Alfred Cartier, *Bibliographie des éditions des de Tournes imprimeurs lyonnais*, 2 vols. (Paris: Editions des Bibliothèques Nationales de France, 1937).

2. Natalis Rondot, *Bernard Salomon peintre et tailleur d'histoires à Lyon, au XVIe siècle* (Lyon: Imprimerie Mougin-Rusand, 1897).

The Roman poet Ovid (43 B.C.-A.D. 17/18) is probably best known for the *Metamorphoses*, his magnificent work combining Greek and Roman mythological themes into a series of stories about the gods and humans and their transformations which are echoed in the transformations of all forms of life. Ovid's writing, with its humanity and delightful sensual quality, has retained its appeal over the centuries, and his superb pictorial allusions have served as inspiration to countless painters, sculptors, and engravers.

The printer of this *Metamorphoses* was Jean de Tournes of Lyons (1504-1564).[1] The Ovid of 1557 is among his finest work, distinguished for its typography, initial letters, decorative borders exhibiting the full range of Mannerist ornament, and the incomparable small-scale woodcut illustrations. Although the cuts are not signed, they are universally attributed to Bernard Salomon (1506/1510-1561), called le petit Bernard, who was de Tournes's chief illustrator.[2] Salomon's tiny compositions reveal the influence of the School of Fontainebleau, with lively elegant figures, full of motion, set in vivid and extensive landscapes.

The edition of 1559 is an Italian translation from the French by Gabriele Simeoni (1509-1575), a minor Italian literary figure. The captions are printed in roman letter and Simeoni's verse is in italic, probably cut by Robert Granjon (d. 1579), the distinguished Parisian type designer.

The series of borders for the illustrations ranges from black-on-white and white-on-black arabesques to nine different historiated, grotesque, or Boschian frames. Some of these had previously been used and many would appear in later de Tournes volumes.

In this edition the illustrations for the tale of Diana and Actaeon (for the story and another treatment of the subject see cat. no. 20) are bordered by exuberant Rabelaisian motifs combined with Renaissance versions of classical herms and putti. The format of caption, picture, and accompanying verse is somewhat reminiscent of an emblem book.

Salomon's finesse in creating a miniature world is clearly shown by the illustration. The hilly, lightly wooded landscape on the left is contrasted with Diana's shaded pool among the reeds. The faintest of shadows on her face might indicate a blush as she splashes water on the hapless hunter, now well on his way to becoming a stag. On the facing page, the helplessness of the dying stag beset by his own hounds is revealed in his half-closed eye and limp, flailing legs. The border of the illustrations contains, among other creatures, an elephant, an ostrich, a swan and cygnets, and a grotesque man-windmill. The entire book is a feast for the eye, a splendid Renaissance interpretation of classical themes.

S.S.G.

Ateone mutato in Cerbio da Diana.

42

Dalla sete e'l calor cacciando vinto
Cerca Ateon pel bosco vna fontana,
Hallo il suo fier destino in parte spinto,
Che mal per lui vi troua entro Diana.
La Dea, col viso di vergogna tinto,
Gli muta in cerbio la sembianza humana,
Et dice, nel gettar quell' onda cruda,
Non lice à ognun veder Diana ignuda.

6. FEDERICO GRISONE

Künstlicher Bericht und aller-
zierlichste Beschreybung . . .
wie die Streitbarn Pferdt . . .
zum Ernst und ritterlicher
kurtzweil geschickt und vol-
kommen zumachen. Augsburg:
Michael Manger in Verlegung
Georgen Willers, 1570. [20], 235,
[43] p., [1] folded leaf of plates. Page
size: 11½ x 7¾ in. (282 x 197 mm.)
Binding: Full 18th-century mottled
calf gilt. Bookplate: William
Davignon. Robert Sterling Clark
Collection.

ILLUSTRATIONS: Title page with
elaborated historiated woodcut border,
1 double-page and 88 full-page woodcuts.

REFERENCES: Rosenwald 707.

NOTES:

1. For a catalogue raisonné of Jost
Amman's work and attribution of
these cuts, see Andreas Andresen, *Jost
Amman, 1539-1591: Graphiker und
Buchillustrator der Renaissance* (1864;
reprint, Amsterdam: G. W. Hissink,
1973).

2. Walter Liedtke, *The Royal Horse and
Rider: Painting, Sculpture and Horseman-
ship 1500-1800* (New York: Abaris
Books in association with The
Metropolitan Museum of Art, 1989),
21, 89.

3. For a description of the edition of
1580, see *Katalog der Freiherrlich von
Lipperheide'schen Kostümbibliothek*,
2 vols. (1896-1905; reprint, New
York: Hacker Art Books, 1963),
2:404, no. 2893.

Freely adapted and enlarged from the Neapolitan nobleman Federico Grisone's *Ordini di cavalcare* (Prescriptions for Training Horses), originally published in 1550, this is the first German edition of that classic treatise. Not only was it reissued in several Italian versions, it was rapidly translated into French, Spanish, and English. A German adaption by Johann Fayser was subsequently reissued three times, evidence of the importance attached in the sixteenth century to the equestrian arts.

The work deals not only with schooling horses but contains extensive instructions and numerous illustrations on the customary types of combat in tournaments at the time of the Emperor Maximilian I (1459-1519). In addition, it portrays and discusses different kinds of bits and bridles and includes a double-page diagram of the parts of a horse. There are also occasional snatches of music, no doubt used to induce horse and rider to perform properly.

Jost Amman (1539-1591) has been proposed as the designer of the woodcuts. Of Swiss origin, he moved to Germany some time before 1560. He probably did not cut his own blocks and is best known for his designs for book illustrations, elaborate ornaments, and emblematic title pages. His name is most closely associated with that of the Frankfurt printer Sigismund Feyerabend (1527/1528-1590) for whom he illustrated the famous *Ständebuch* (1568), a manual of crafts and trades with rhymes by Hans Sachs.[1]

With the possible exception of the frontispiece, the cuts in the Grisone book do not, however, exhibit the facility of those of the *Ständebuch*; indeed, they appear to be copied from the Naples edition of 1550.[2] They are far more schematic and lack the modeling or sense of depth Amman usually achieved. A more plausible suggestion is that the illustrations of knights found in this book were used by Amman as a model for his *Ritterliche Reutter Kunst* (Frankfurt, 1584).[3]

The frontispiece of the *Künstlicher Bericht* is typical of German books of the late sixteenth century, in which an elaborate ornamental frame of strapwork shaded to achieve dimensionality is pierced by swags of fruit and by openings filled with mythological and historical warriors and their horses. It contrasts strikingly with the greater simplicity of the rest of the book's illustrations, decorative initials, and tailpieces.

The illustration shown depicts a horse and rider performing one of the school movements. While the rider somewhat resembles a stuffed doll, the horse is represented with great verve. The vigorous, forceful outlines and minimal shading of the figures are an apt accompaniment to the bold black letter and calligraphic initials. This sense of balance of the page is evident throughout the book, thus making it a handsome example of German Renaissance typography and illustration.

S.S.G.

7. ANTOINE DE PLUVINEL

L'instruction du roy, en l'exercice
de monter a cheval par messire
Antoine de Pluvinel. . . . Paris: Michel
Nivelle, 1625. [16], 207 p., [62]
folded leaves of plates. Page size:
14 x 9⁵⁄₁₆ in. (356 x 233 mm.)
Binding: Full contemporary mottled
calf gilt. Bookplate: Ph[ilip]
Honywood of Marks Hall. Robert
Sterling Clark Collection.

ILLUSTRATIONS: Added double-page
engraved title page, 3 engraved portraits, 61 double-page engravings by
Crispijn de Passe II, and 1 engraved
portrait of Pluvinel by Simon de
Passe; 1 unrelated page of geometric
figures bound in following p. 206.

REFERENCES: Brunet IV, 749; Brunet
Suppl. 261-262.

NOTES:

1. For a description of the 1623 edition,
see Mellon 21 and *Hollstein's Dutch and
Flemish Etchings, Engravings and Woodcuts, ca. 1450-1700*, K. G. Boon, ed.
vol. 16 (Amsterdam: M. Hertzberger,
1949-) 16: 138-139, no. 175.

2. Daniel Franken, *L'oeuvre gravé des van
de Passe* (Amsterdam: F. Muller, 1881).

3. Walter Liedtke, *The Royal Horse and
Rider: Painting, Sculpture and Horseman-
ship 1500-1800* (New York: Abaris
Books in association with The
Metropolitan Museum of Art, 1989),
21-22.

The book of instruction on horsemanship by Antoine de Pluvinel (1555-1620) was written in the form of a dialogue between Pluvinel, Louis XIII's instructor in equitation, and the young king. The book is typical of an aristocratic taste for festivals and ceremonies, combined with an elaborate display of the equestrian and martial arts.

The engravings depict the king, his courtiers and servants, as well as the horses and their trappings at Pluvinel's academy of equitation. Used previously in the 1623 edition of the same book entitled *Maneige royal*, the prints were designed and engraved by Crispijn de Passe II (c. 1597-c. 1670).[1] De Passe was a member of a peripatetic family of prolific engravers of Netherlandish origin who worked for a time in Utrecht.[2] His father, Crispijn de Passe I (1565-1637), had made illustrations for the Plantin Press in Antwerp. Crispijn II lived and worked in Paris from about 1617 to 1630, and the plates for this book were made there under Pluvinel's supervision between 1617 and 1620.[3]

In addition to the illustrations in the text, this volume has a typically Baroque added title page consisting of a stage-like setting flanked by the figures of Minerva (Scientia, or Knowledge) and Hercules (Robur, or Strength), each leading a horse. Four engraved portraits precede the text; that of Pluvinel was engraved by Simon de Passe (1595-1647), Crispijn II's brother. Each of the text plates is set within a fanciful architectural framework of pillars and entablature, abundantly decorated with swags, putti, coats of arms, harnesses, curry combs, or other equine references. In the foreground, a pattern of horses' hooves frequently appears in the dust. In all there are six such frames which are repeated throughout the text, and six of the illustrations are used twice.

Many of the individuals portrayed, including the grooms, are identi-fied by name, with Pluvinel—bearing a striking resemblance to Henri IV, the king's father—figuring prominently in most of the scenes. All of the figures are elaborately costumed and placed within architectural or land-scape backgrounds, the focal point in each instance being the horse as it performs the complicated maneuvers of the school figures or the tourna-ment. Several plates have no figure compositions but portray bits and saddles for the horse, and habits and whips for the rider. The entire book is an exuberant and sumptuous portrayal of the finest arts of horsemanship from an age when mastery of equitation had become a metaphor for the successful exercise of public power.

In the illustration shown, the central figure of the young king on horseback faces M. de Pluvinel on the right. Courtiers, a stable boy, and pikemen are grouped on the left. The background trees and architecture are more lightly engraved to enhance the sense of recession. Light and shade play across the foreground, especially on the burnished flanks of the horse as he turns a surprisingly winsome glance toward the viewer.

S.S.G.

8. PIERRE CORNEILLE

La mort de Pompee tragedie.
Paris: Antoine de Sommaville et
Augustin Courbé, 1644. [14],
100 p., [1] leaf of plates. Page size:
8¹¹⁄₁₆ x 6½ in. (226 x 165 mm.)
Binding: Full red morocco by Allô.
Robert Sterling Clark Collection.

ILLUSTRATIONS: Added engraved title
page by François Chauveau.

REFERENCES: Brunet II, 285.

NOTES:

1. Jules Le Petit, *Bibliographie des principales éditions originales d'écrivains
français du XVᵉ au XVIIIᵉ siècle* (Paris:
Maison Quantin, 1888), 160.

2. For an extensive catalogue of
Chauveau's works, see Roger-Armand
Wiegert, *Inventaire du fonds français:
graveurs du XVIIᵉ siècle*, 7 vols. (Paris:
Bibliothèque Nationale, 1939-1976),
2: 393-560.

La mort de Pompée was a dramatization by Pierre Corneille (1606-1684), the great classical French dramatist, of events connected with major figures in Roman history. He used the story primarily to meditate upon the downfall of human greatness. The play opens with the assassination of Pompey by Ptolemy's minions over the objections of the latter's sister Cleopatra. Fearing that Cleopatra will be placed on the throne, Ptolemy then proposes to assassinate Caesar, who has come to Egypt to avenge Pompey's death. Pompey's widow Cornelia reveals the conspiracy to Caesar, Ptolemy is killed in battle, and Cleopatra is indeed crowned.

The play was first presented near the beginning of the year 1643 by the Comédiens du Marais and was printed shortly thereafter with a *privilège*, or license to print, which unfortunately for Corneille did not represent copyright as we know it today. Other theatrical troupes undertook it over his protests, but custom allowed plays that had been printed to be produced freely without payment of royalties. It was quite popular and from 1680 to 1876, 192 representations were held at the Théatre Français.[1]

The added engraved title page signed "F. C." is the work of François Chauveau (1613-1676).[2] A pupil of Laurent de la Hyre, he produced plates after his master, as well as after Poussin and Eustache Lesueur, all major painters of the French Baroque. Enjoying a high reputation among his contemporaries, Chauveau is estimated to have produced about three thousand plates, which often illustrated the writings of major seventeenth-century authors such as Scudéry, Scarron, Corneille, Racine, Molière, and La Fontaine.

The elaborate title page depicts the death of Pompey as he is attacked in a boat by the assassins. The Roman soldiers on the left, striking poses derived ultimately from classical sculpture, form a frame and lead the eye to the major event in the middle ground. In the background is a small landscape view topped by impending storm clouds. The agitated sea emphasizes the drama, and the expressive use of a white void for the water in the background further highlights the scene.

S.S.G.

F.C. In. et fecit.

LA. MORT. DE. POMPÉE.

A. PARIS.

Chez. A. De. Sommauille. & . A. Courbé.
Au. palles. 1644.

9. C. Julius Caesar

La guerre des Suisses, traduit du
I. livre des Commentaires de Iule
Cesar, par Louys XIV, Dieu-donné roy
de France & de Navarre. Paris:
Imprimerie Royale, 1651. [2], 18 p.,
[4] folded leaves of plates. Page size:
15 x 9¾ in. (381 x 248 mm.) Binding: 18th-century full red morocco
gilt, with arms of Louis XIV.
Bookplate of Edouard Rahir. Robert
Sterling Clark Collection.

ILLUSTRATIONS: Title page vignette
arms of France, historiated initial,
tailpiece, 4 double-page engravings
by L. Richer;[1] plate after p. 14 signed
"N. Cochin"; after p. 16 attributed to
Abraham Bosse.

REFERENCES: Brunet I, 1460; Rahir
1002; Rosenwald 1397.

NOTES:

1. The second plate is signed "L. Richer
sc." It is probable that he engraved
the other plates as well.

2. For an extensive list of Cochin's prints,
see Roger-Armand Wiegert, *Inventaire
du fonds français: graveurs du XVIIe
siècle*, 7 vols. (Paris: Bibliothèque
Nationale, 1939-1976), 3: 18-76.

3. For an extensive list of Bosse's prints,
see ibid., 1: 471-534.

The primary interest in the text of this translation of the first book of Caesar's *Commentaries* (The War against the Swiss [Helvetii]) is that it was made by the young King Louis XIV when he was thirteen years old. The edition itself, however, is a sumptuous one, with four double-page engravings, two of which are attributed to Nicolas Cochin (1610-1686)[2] and Abraham Bosse[3] (1602-1676). In addition, it was printed at the recently founded Imprimerie Royale. In 1640 Cardinal Richelieu had established this printing house in the Louvre with the mission of setting standards for typography, engraving, and paper. The Imprimerie exists to this day, having been renamed the Imprimerie Nationale after 1871. In the latter half of the seventeenth century some superb book illustrators and decorators were associated with the Imprimerie, among them Claude Mellan, François Chauveau, and Abraham Bosse.

Bosse was a prolific engraver specializing in scenes of everyday life of the lesser nobility and bourgeoisie. A Calvinist, he also revealed great originality in religious iconography, clothing the protagonists of biblical scenes in contemporary fashion. He illustrated books on architecture, theater, science, and literature and produced numerous engraved portraits. He is also known for his interest in perspective and most importantly for his book on the method of copper-plate engraving, *Traité des manières de graver en taille-douce. . . .* First published in 1645, it was reprinted several times after his death and remained influential for many years.

Nicolas Cochin was a member of a large family of artists originating in Troyes. He was influenced by Sebastien Le Clerc (see cat. no. 12) and Jacques Callot. François Chauveau (see cat. nos. 8 and 10) was one of his pupils. Cochin excelled in small-scale compositions, rather like Callot, and specialized in scenes of sieges, encampments, and battles.

In the illustration of the Ordonnance of the two armies, Cochin captured in miniature the great sweep of the battlefield with Caesar's phalanxes lined up against the Swiss. The curious tilted perspective augments the sense of vastness in which individuals become ants. Skillful use of light and shade prevent the composition from becoming monotonous.

S.S.G.

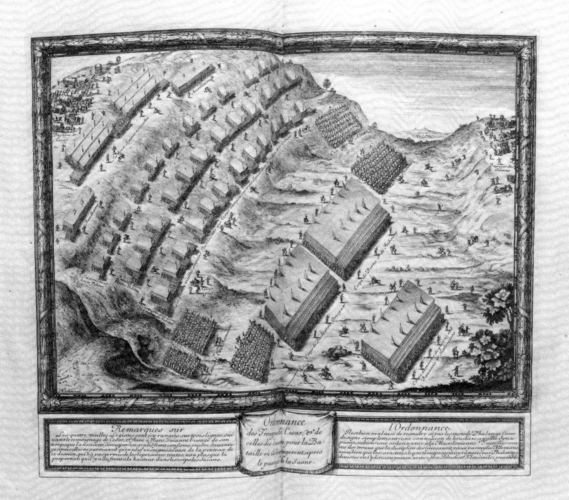

10. PIERRE CORNEILLE

Andromede tragedie représentée avec les machines sur le Theatre Royal de Bourbon. Rouen: Laurens Maurry; se vendent à Paris: Charles de Sercy, 1651. [10], 123, [1] p., [7] leaves of plates (6 folded). Page size: 8⅜ x 6⅜ in. (217 x 164 mm.) Binding: Full red morocco by Cuzin. Robert Sterling Clark Collection.

ILLUSTRATIONS: Added engraved title page and 6 folded plates. The added title page and the first, second, fifth, and sixth plates are signed by François Chauveau.

REFERENCES: Brunet Suppl. 311.[1]

NOTES:

1. The work is also listed and the plates described in Emile Picot's *Bibliographie cornélienne. . . .* (Paris: A. Fontaine, 1876), 63.

2. See, for example, Jules Le Petit, *Bibliographie des principales éditions originales d'écrivains français du XVe au XVIIIe siècle* (Paris: Maison Quantin, 1888), 172; Marie-Françoise Christout, *Le Ballet de Cour de Louis XIV, 1643-1672* (Paris: J. Picard, 1967), 47-51, 54-55; and Per Bjurström, *Giacomo Torelli and Baroque Stage Design* (Stockholm: Almqvist & Wiksell, 1962).

Corneille's *Andromède*, originally set to music, is a play with mechanical devices. The type of play in which machines are used to transport actors about the stage producing spectacular effects has its roots in the medieval theater, court ballet, and Italian drama. It was traditional that such "machine" plays be based on mythological themes. In this one, when Casseopeia boasts of her daughter Andromeda's beauty, a contest for the latter's hand ensues between Perseus and Phineus. After Perseus kills a monster, Andromeda chooses him. Following the standard intervention from the gods, Corneille has the whole family translated to the heavens to conform with the fact that four constellations bear their names.

The play has a curious history.[2] Cardinal Mazarin imported an opera/ballet, *Orfeo* by Luigi Rossi, from Italy, hoping to introduce the genre to France and incidentally to amuse the nine-year-old Louis XIV. It had a certain success and Mazarin thereupon commissioned Corneille to write something in French, but constrained him to use the scenery that had been designed for *Orfeo* by Giacomo Torelli (1608-1678), the Italian stage designer, engineer, and architect. Torelli was renowned for introducing a new technique of machinery which could change a whole set in one operation. The music for *Andromède* was composed by Charles Dassoucy (1605-1677), a French satirical poet, lutenist, and composer. Corneille began work on the play in 1647, but production was postponed due to the illness of the king and the civil war known as the *Fronde*.

Andromède was first performed in the Salle du Petit-Bourbon at the beginning of the year 1650, and, according to the colophon, this printed edition was completed 13 August 1651. A subsequent production of 1682 was noteworthy as the first time a live horse, playing Pegasus, was seen on the stage in France.

Corneille himself stated that this play was "only for the eyes," so the illustrations of the text, based on Torelli's sets, assume great importance. The added title page and three of the scenes were engraved by François Chauveau, whose illustrations ornamented most of the important French literature of the second and third quarter of the century (see also cat. no. 8). There is no reason to suspect that Chauveau did not engrave all the plates, as the technique is consistent. The first plate also bears the caption "Berdot de Montbelliard pinx." Berdot may well have translated the sets into small pictures for the engraver of all six plates.

The plate for the setting of the third act shows Perseus astride the winged horse Pegasus. They attack the dragon threatening Andromeda, who is stranded on the rocks at the right. Agitated spectators gesticulate on the left. The framing rocks converging toward the vanishing point accentuate the drama and help focus attention on the actors. The whole scene is one of great verve and must surely have delighted the young king.

S.S.G.

11. JEAN GALBERT DE CAMPISTRON

Acis et Galatée, pastorale heroique en musique. Représentée pour la premiere fois dans le Château d'Anet devant Monseigneur le Dauphin, par l'Academie Royale de Musique. Paris: Christophe Ballard, 1686. [8], 41, [7] p., [1] leaf of plates. *There is a typographical error in page numbering: p. 27 is misnumbered 35.* Page size: 9 x 7 in. (178 x 229 mm.) Binding: Contemporary red morocco gilt with arms of Louis Alexandre de Bourbon, Comte de Toulouse.[1] Label of the Charles Giraud sale, Paris, 1855, lot 1816; bookplate of Edouard Rahir. Robert Sterling Clark Collection.

ILLUSTRATION: Engraved frontispiece by Dolivar after I. Berin.

REFERENCES: Rahir 998.

NOTES:

1. The Comte de Toulouse was the son of Louis XIV and Mme de Montespan.

2. For a catalogue raisonné of Berain's works, see Roger-Armand Weigert, *Jean I Berain: dessinateur de la Chambre et du Cabinet du Roi*, 2 vols. (Paris: Les Editions d'Art et d'Histoire, 1937). The frontispiece of *Acis* is described in vol. 2, p. 120, no. 38, as being known in only one state.

3. For the activities of the Ballard family, see Philippe Rénouard, *Répertoire des imprimeurs parisiens, libraires, fondeurs de caractères et correcteurs d'imprimerie. . . .* (Paris: M. J. Minard, 1965).

*A*cis et Galatée was the first play to be produced by Jean Galbert de Campistron (1656-1723). A pastorale with music composed by Jean Baptiste Lully (1623-1687), it was prepared for a fête held at the château of Anet for the Dauphin, son of Louis XIV. The play was a success, and Campistron became France's principal playwright after the retirement of Jean Racine. Largely forgotten today, Campistron nevertheless possessed a sound theatrical instinct, if not the originality of Racine, and echoes of Corneille's proud and tragic heroines are found in his work.

The narrative of the play is a simple one. Acis, a shepherd from Sicily and son of Pan, and Galatea are lovers, but she is pursued by the one-eyed giant Polyphemus. Polyphemus surprises the couple in a grotto and crushes Acis with a huge boulder, whereupon Galatea leaps into the water. Neptune, in response to her prayers, changes Acis into a river so that the lovers will be together and enjoy happiness forever.

The artist of the frontispiece, Jean Berain I (1640-1711), was best known for his ornamental designs and as the creator of an entire decorative style. After 1680 he was the principal designer for the Académie Royale de Musique, and following the death of Charles Le Brun in 1690 he became the official decorator of the court. In that capacity he designed everything, from furniture to carriages, boats, clocks, ballet costumes, banquets, and fireworks displays, most of which were recorded in engravings. He also designed a number of frontispieces primarily for opera librettos. About five hundred of these various prints survive, although most were actually engraved by other hands.[2]

The printer of the play, Christophe Ballard (c. 1641-1715), was probably the great-grandson of Robert Ballard I, who was named by Henri II as music printer to the king. The family dynasty retained this privilege and remained important in the world of music printing until the Revolution.[3]

While the typography and layout of *Acis et Galatée* are far from notable—the type seems to be worn and the borders do not relate very well to the text—the frontispiece is full of verve and is an appropriate introduction to the action of the play. It depicts the climax of the drama with a grand sense of theatricality. The strong curvilinear sweep from the menacing giant on the left is firmly anchored by the trees on the right. The landscape suggests the stage setting as it recedes into the distance, while the goats and sheep grazing on the hill above Polyphemus provide the necessary pastoral background. A note of high drama is evident in the overwrought gestures of the characters and in the sharp contrasts of light and shade. The scene is tempered, however, by the confining architectural frame, the serenity of the seated allegorical figures at the bottom, and the putti holding their heavy flower garlands and the arms of France. The little scene seems to exemplify the French Baroque, in which a tension often exists between formal and flamboyant elements.

S.S.G.

ACIS ET
GALATEE

J. Berin In et del.   Doluar. Fecit

12. CHARLES PERRAULT AND
ISAAC DE BENSERADE

Labyrinte de Versailles. Suivant
la copie à Paris de l'Imprimerie
Royale, 1693. [Amsterdam: Pierre
Mortier.] [10], 78, [2] p. Page size:
6¼ x 8 in. (203 x 159 mm.) Binding:
Contemporary vellum. Robert
Sterling Clark Collection.

ILLUSTRATIONS: Engraved title page,
vignette on printed title page, 41
engraved plates.

NOTES:

1. The Amsterdam edition is briefly
described in Maxime Préaud,
*Inventaire du fonds français: graveurs du
XVIIᵉ siècle, Sebastien Le Clerc*, 2 vols.
(Paris: Bibliothèque Nationale, 1980),
2: 212. The entire series of plates from
the Paris edition is reproduced and
described, nos. 1818-1858,
pp. 211-221.

2. For a description of the original
labyrinth and some translated excerpts
from Perrault's text, see Robert
W. Berger, *In the Gardens of the Sun
King* (Washington, D. C.: Dumbarton
Oaks Research Library and Collection,
1985), 29-40.

The *Labyrinte de Versailles* has been described as a guidebook and there is evidence that it was used as such. The book was first published in 1677 and again in 1679 with prose descriptions by Charles Perrault (1628-1703), who is perhaps best known today for his collections of fairy tales. The verses are by Isaac de Benserade (1613-1691), poet, dramatist, and creator of spectacles for the court of Louis XIV. The Clark book is an adaptation of this work and was printed in Amsterdam in 1693 by Pierre Mortier, the great international publisher of illustrated books. Perrault's introduction is not included.[1]

The illustrations, originally by Sebastien Le Clerc (1637-1714), were copied rather faithfully but were changed by the addition of people in costumes of the court and extended on each side by the addition of foliage or garden elements. Each plate, with the exception of the frontispiece, the map of the labyrinth, and the first illustration depicting the king himself at the entrance to the labyrinth, represents one of the fountains. The fountains were probably designed by Charles Le Brun (1619-1690), the most celebrated French painter and designer of the century. The original layout of the garden was the work of André Le Nôtre (1613-1700), the distinguished architect and landscape designer. The labyrinth was begun about 1666, finished in 1673/1674, and survived until 1775 when it was replaced by the Bosquet de la Reine (Queen's Wood).[2]

Sebastien Le Clerc, a draftsman, engraver, and writer, was also a major book illustrator of the second half of the seventeenth century. His originality, vitality, and ability to capture a moment have much in common with Jacques Callot (1592/1593-1635) who, like Le Clerc, originated in Lorraine. Le Clerc's small-scale, graceful illustrations contributed to the development of the elegant Rococo vignette, which enjoyed such favor in the eighteenth century. The anonymous plates of the Amsterdam book do not have quite the delicacy or sense of intimacy of Le Clerc's originals, nor the subtle contrasts of light and shadow. Nevertheless, they are lively and retain much of the charm of the originals.

The illustration shown depicts one of the fountains, The Council of the Rats. The rats discussed means of escape from the depredations of the cat, resulting in a proposal to bell the cat. This advice was well received, but the difficulty was that no one wanted to do it. In a leafy wood, around a little basin, several rats are seated: one larger than the others is in the center holding the bell; all spout jets of water. The promenading spectators contribute to an evocation of the delights of the gardens of the Sun King.

S.S.G.

Le Conseil des Rats, dans le Labirinte de Versailles.

25

13. COLEN CAMPBELL

Vitruvius Britannicus, or The British architect, containing the plans, elevations, and sections of the regular buildings, both publick and private, in Great Britain. . . . London: sold by the author . . . and Joseph Smith, 1715-1725. 3 vols. in 2. Vol. 1/2: 10 p., [86] leaves of plates (some folded)/8 p., [73] leaves of plates (some folded); vol. 3: 12 p., [74] leaves of plates (some folded). Page size: Vol. 1/2, 17½ x 11⅝ in. (445 x 295 mm.); vol. 3, 17³⁄₁₆ x 11³⁄₁₆ in. (437 x 284 mm.) Binding: Vol. 1/2, full mottled calf; vol. 3, ¼ calf. Bookplate in vol. 1/2 with initials EHLK; in vol. 3, bookplates of R. Townley Parker and Reginald Arthur Tatton. Robert Sterling Clark Collection.

ILLUSTRATIONS: Vol. 1/2: 157 engraved plates; vol. 3: 74 engraved plates. While most of the elevations and many of the other illustrations were based on designs by Campbell, many are unidentified. In vol. 1 the engraver is unidentified; in vols. 2 and 3 most of the plates were engraved by Hulsberg, the remaining are unidentified.

REFERENCES: Fowler 76.[1]

NOTES:

1. Fowler 76 includes additional, later volumes.

2. Howard E. Stutchbury, *The Architecture of Colen Campbell* (Manchester: Manchester University Press, 1967), 145.

3. Colen Campbell, *Vitruvius Britannicus*, 1:1.

4. Ibid., 2.

5. Ibid., 3:2.

6. For a thorough treatment of the publication of *Vitruvius Britannicus*, see T. P. Connor, "The making of 'Vitruvius Britannicus,'" *Architectural History* 20 (1977): 14-30.

When Colen Campbell (1676-1729) published the first volume of *Vitruvius Britannicus* in 1715, only one building of his design had been built and another was just underway.[2] And yet, in this first volume he illustrated designs for six buildings (although only one of these was ever built). Campbell placed himself in good company by including, along with his own designs, those of such well-known British architects of the seventeenth century as Inigo Jones and Sir Christopher Wren, as well as designs by the already accomplished "competitor" of Campbell, John Vanbrugh. In short, *Vitruvius Britannicus* advertised the work of a relatively unknown architect.

In the publication Campbell associated himself with a new stylistic development as well as with more important architects. *Vitruvius Britannicus* was avant garde in its criticism of the Baroque, in its appeal to Palladian principles, and in its revival of interest in the work of Inigo Jones. In the introduction, Palladio is credited with having "surpass'd his Contemporaries. . . . And indeed, this excellent Architect seems to have arrived at a Ne plus ultra of his Art."[3] Yet Campbell sees in the works of Inigo Jones "all the Regularity of the former [Palladio], with an Addition of Beauty and Majesty, in which our Architect is esteemed to have out-done all that went before. . . ."[4] By stressing Jones's achievements in this large and impressive publication, Campbell coupled his own name with the great Palladian of the seventeenth century and also underscored the significance of British architects in the development of a modern style.

Shown here is one of the beautiful engravings of Mereworth Castle (vol. 3, p. 37), in which Campbell's Palladianism is particularly apparent; in fact, the architect clearly acknowledges the Villa Rotonda, built for Paolo Almerico, as his source: "I shall not pretend to say, That I have made any improvements in this Plan from that of *Palladio*, for *Signor Almerico*. . . ."[5] Although freely adjusting the proportions, dome design, and internal room divisions, he took directly from Palladio the square plan, the hexastyle Ionic porticoes on each of the four sides, and the plain, stuccoed surfaces. Begun in 1722, Mereworth Castle was the first full-blown Palladian building in Great Britain.[6]

J.D.W.

a Scale of 60 feet

10   20   30   40   50   60

Extends 120 feet

The Elevation of Mereworth Castle near Maidstone in Kent
the Seat of the Honourable John Fane Esq.

Co: Campbell Architectus   H. Hulsbergh Sculp.

14. LONGUS

Les amours pastorales de Daphnis et Chloé. [Paris: Quillau], 1718. [12], 164 p., [33] leaves of plates. Page size: 6 9/16 x 4 in. (167 x 102 mm.) Tipped in are two folded manuscript sheets: one is a lengthy statement "fait à Paris ce la Décembre 1790" and signed "Debure L'aîné Libraire de la Bibliotheque du Roi"; the other a "Copié sur le projet ecrit de la main de S.A.R. l'an 1712." Binding: Full green morocco gilt, pink silk gilt doublures and flyleaves, by C. Kalthoeber. Robert Sterling Clark Collection.

ILLUSTRATIONS: Engraved title page by Audran after A. Coypel, engraved headpiece by Scotin, 28 plates engraved by Audran after Philippe d'Orléans. Bound in are 3 engraved impressions of the "Petits pieds" plate attributed to the Comte de Caylus and lettered "Conclusion du Roman": a regular impression, one in sanguine, and the third a counterproof. Also bound in is a fourth engraving of the "Petits pieds" subject, but it differs in design from the typical one: it is unlettered, the grotto's edge is more intricately defined, the nearer cupid's head is in profile, and overall it is a harsher design with greater contrast. Tipped in on the last page of text, p. 164, is an engraved portrait of the translator Amyot by St. Aubin lettered "Aug. St. Aubin sculp./1803."

REFERENCES: Cohen-de Ricci 648-651; Ray 2.

Longus wrote his pastoral in Greek sometime in the second or third century A.D., but it was Jacques Amyot's French translation of 1559 that has made the work so popular. The delightful love story about a shepherd and shepherdess attracted many artists and has frequently been published in lavish editions. (See cat. nos. 41 and 42 for important twentieth-century examples.)

For this early eighteenth-century edition, Prince Philippe d'Orléans (1674-1723), Louis XIV's nephew, made a series of designs illustrating Longus's text under the guidance of Antoine Coypel (1661-1722) in 1714. These designs, plus a title page designed by Coypel, were then engraved by Benoit Audran I (1661-1721) and published with text in 1718. It is not, however, the illustrations (the example illustrated here is opposite p. 20) that make this edition desirable to collectors, but rather the royal pedigree (the book was even published during Philippe d'Orléans's regency) and its relevance to the long series of illustrated editions of *Daphnis et Chloé*.

The Clark copy is particularly interesting because it contains a number of items that were not a part of the original 1718 publication. The inclusion of four extra prints (one a counterproof) attributed to the Comte de Caylus (1692-1765) and the portrait of Amyot by St.-Aubin (1736-1807) are just the kind of thing a book collector finds of value. But even more interesting, this copy contains a lengthy statement written by Louis XVI's librarian, Guillaume Debure, in 1790. It describes how he had this very copy made up from sheets of the text and plates which had originally belonged to Philippe d'Orléans's *valet de chambre* and presumably were reserved for the Regent's use, and it further states that he had it bound in England. The Clark copy also contains a handwritten copy of a list of the subjects to be illustrated that had been made by Philippe d'Orléans. These unique features—the added prints, the manuscript material, and the beautiful, signed Neoclassical binding—confer on the basic illustrated text a luster which it would not otherwise deserve.

J.D.W.

Philipus inv. et pinxit 1714.   B.^{tue} Audran sculp.
Chloe prend les habits de Daphnis qui se baigne.

15. DENIS DIDEROT, JEAN
LEROND D'ALEMBERT, ET AL.

Encyclopédie, ou Dictionnaire
raisonné des sciences, des arts et des
métiers, par une societé de gens
de lettres, mis en ordre par
m. Diderot . . . et quant à la partie
mathématique, par m. d'Alembert.
Paris: Briasson, David, LeBreton,
Durand, 1751-1772. 28 vols. of which
11 are plates. (Vols. 8-17 have imprint: Neufchastel: S. Faulche, 1756.)
Supplément á l'Encyclopédie.
Amsterdam: M. M. Rey, 1776-1777.
4 vols. *Suite de recueil de planches.* . . .
Paris: Panckoucke, 1777. 1 vol. *Table
analytique et raisonné des matières.* . . .
Paris: Panckoucke, 1780. 2 vols.[1] Page
size: 15½ x 9¾ in. (395 x 248 mm.)
Binding: Full mottled calf gilt.
Robert Sterling Clark Collection.

ILLUSTRATIONS: 12 volumes of engraved plates, some folded, by various
artists, for a total of 3,129 plates.

REFERENCES: Brunet II, 700-701.

NOTES:

1. The Clark lacks vols. 1-9 of the set.

2. See especially Robert Darnton, *The
   Business of Enlightenment: A Publishing
   History of the Encyclopédie, 1775-1800*
   (Cambridge, Mass: Harvard Univer-
   sity Press, 1979).

3. William Doyle, *The Oxford History of
   the French Revolution* (Oxford:
   Clarendon Press, 1989), 52.

4. The first volume of text was published
   in 1751; volumes 8-17 were published
   in 1765, along with the fourth volume
   of plates under a false imprint. The
   last volumes of plates were issued in
   1772. But also considered part of the
   first edition were the four supplemen-
   tary volumes (1776-1777), the supple-
   mentary volume of plates (1777), and
   the index, or *Tables analytiques* (1780).

The *Encyclopédie* is one of the best known works of the eighteenth century. Studies of its role in the Enlightenment abound, as do those concerning the vicissitudes of its publication.[2] It is said that few works were more important "in promoting the values of independent thinking and indifference to authority."[3] At the same time it represents an affirmation of the possibility of progress and the perfectibility of human institutions through reason.

The great project was begun in 1747 by Denis Diderot (1713-1784) and Jean Lerond d'Alembert (1717-1783). More than a compendium of facts, the *Encyclopédie* ordered knowledge according to philosophic prin-ciples as set forth by d'Alembert in the Preliminary Discourse. An engrav-ing of the Tree of Knowledge illustrates his conception that the arts and sciences derive exclusively from three mental faculties: reason, imagina-tion, and memory. Philosophy forms the trunk of the tree while theology has been relegated to a branch next to black magic.

Diderot enlisted more than two hundred collaborators, including such luminaries as Voltaire and Rousseau, Buffon and Euler, d'Holbach and Turgot—a veritable pantheon of eighteenth-century literary and scientific figures. A promotion campaign was begun in 1750 with the distribution of a prospectus that promised eight volumes of text and two of illustrations to be available to subscribers within two years. It could scarcely have been further from the mark. The edition ultimately stretched to a total of thirty-five volumes and the two years extended to thirty.[4]

The *Encyclopédie* remains a monument to the spirit of the Enlighten-ment. The massive volumes of plates provide us with a comprehensive view of contemporary life and work. In addition, they reflect the interests, and to a certain extent the behavior, of the cultural elite for whom the publica-tion was designed. While the engravings are not artistically distinguished, they are, nonetheless, universally competent in their execution. Details are meticulously portrayed (and labeled). Many of the scenes go well beyond the schematic and are embellished with naturalistic views of town and countryside. A whole world is encompassed in these pages.

We have chosen to exhibit one of the frequently reproduced images not only because it is typical, but because it relates to printing. At the top appears a print shop where two compositors set type, while a third person is imposing the formes, tapping the bars of type with a hammer to make all the letters of equal height. Below the little scene are several schematic diagrams of three lines of type. On the facing page can be seen these three lines as they appear when printed. As a didactic image this plate could scarcely be improved.

S.S.G.

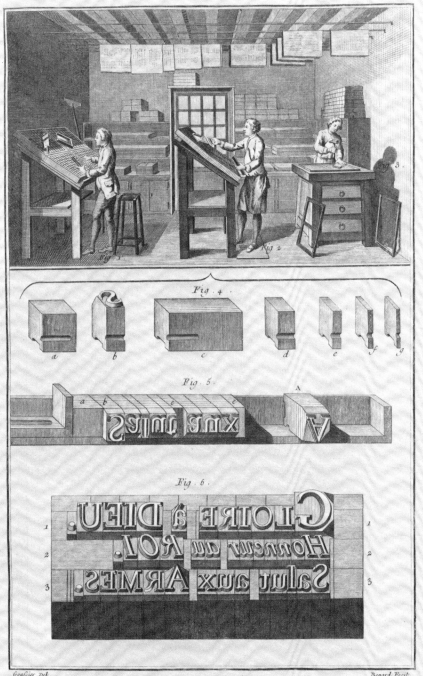

Pl. I.

Goussier Del.   *Benard Fecit.*

Imprimerie en Lettres, L'Operation de la Casse.

16. JEAN DE LA FONTAINE

Fables choises, mises en vers par J. de La Fontaine. Paris: Desaint & Saillant, et Durand, 1755-1759. 4 vols. Vol. 1: [4], xxx, xviii, 124 p., [71] leaves of plates; vol. 2: [4], ii, 135 p., [68] leaves of plates; vol. 3: [4], iv, 146 p., [68] leaves of plates; vol. 4: [4], ii, 188 p., [69] leaves of plates. Page size: 16^{5}/16 x 10^{15}/16 in. (414 x 278 mm.) Binding: Modern 1/4 calf. Purchase 1986.

ILLUSTRATIONS: Except for the added portrait, all the engravings were designed by Oudry. Vol. 1: frontispiece and 70 engraved plates; vol. 2: 68 engraved plates; vol. 3: 68 engraved plates; vol. 4: 69 engraved plates. (See Ray 5 for a list of the engravers represented in each volume.) Wood engravings by Le Seur and Papillon after Bachelier: title-page vignette repeated in each volume, 1 headpiece and 5 tailpieces in vol. 1, and a tailpiece following many of the fables in the 4 vols. Added to vol. 1 is an engraved portrait of Oudry by Tardieu after Largillière. The Clark copy contains the second state of the first plate for fable CLXXII.[1] Most of the plates in vol. 4 are on pale blue paper. Although this suggests late impressions, on the whole the impressions in all 4 vols. are fairly good.

REFERENCES: Cohen-de Ricci 548-550; Ray 5.

NOTES:

1. For a thorough examination of the etched states and a description of the making of this edition of La Fontaine's *Fables*, see Marquis de Girodin, "L'édition des fables dite d'Oudry de La Fontaine," *Bulletin du bibliophile* (1913): 217-236, 277-292, 330-347, 386-398.

2. The contributions of the major artists and wood engravers are discussed in La Fontaine, "Advertissement de l'éditeur," *Fables choises*, iii-viii.

Jean de La Fontaine's (1621-1695) fables, based on both ancient and modern sources, were first published between 1668 and 1694. Their lighthearted and gentle tone, endearing to both children and adults, insured their immediate popularity and has encouraged countless editions in the three hundred years since they were first written. In the eighteenth century alone, there were three editions of the *Fables* containing beautiful illustrations.

The first of these, and the most lavish, was this 1755-1759 edition containing illustrations designed by Jean Baptiste Oudry (1686-1755). Because the original drawings, made for his own amusement, date between 1729 and 1734, the illustrations have a late Baroque, early Rococo flavor which contrasts sharply with the high Rococo engravings by Fessard in a 1765-1775 edition. With Oudry's loose sketches in hand, Charles Nicolas Cochin the younger (1715-1790) produced a set of finished drawings suitable for the engravers to copy and then took charge of the production of the illustrations. Since there were 276 illustrations by more than forty engravers and a large number of wood-engraved fleurons, it is not surprising that the publication took several years to complete.[2]

Oudry's designs provide a whole world for La Fontaine's characters. In many of the illustrations, the animals act in a fully realized rural landscape which domesticates and humanizes the fables. In Fable III of the first book (vol. 1, facing p. 6), which is about a frog who explodes in an attempt to make himself bigger than the ox, Oudry's setting includes a gatepost in the foreground, farm buildings in the middle distance, and a simple tower in the background. This illustration, as the small lettering just below the image tells us, was invented by Oudry, the initial design was etched by Cochin, and the plate was then finished with the burin (an engraving tool) by Gaillart. For the fleurons (there is a lovely one on the page facing this illustration), two more artists—the designer and the craftsman who cut the block—are represented. This publication, with its large number of engraved plates and decorative wood engravings and involving the expertise of so many artists and craftsmen, has remained one of the most admired editions of La Fontaine's *Fables*.

J.D.W.

LA GRENOUILLE QUI SE VEUT FAIRE AUSSI GROSSE QUE LE BŒUF. Fable III.

17. GIOVANNI BOCCACCIO

Il decamerone. . . . Londra [i.e., Paris: Prault], 1757. 5 vols. Vol. 1: xi, 292 p., [24] leaves of plates; vol. 2: 271 p., [23] leaves of plates; vol. 3: 195 p., [23] leaves of plates; vol. 4: 161 [i.e., 261] p., [23] leaves of plates; vol. 5: 247 p., [23] leaves of plates. Page size: 8⅜ x 5³⁄₁₆ in. (214 x 131 mm.) Binding: ¼ red calf. Purchase 1985.

ILLUSTRATIONS: Gravelot designed 89 of the 111 plates, the 5 title pages, and all 98 tailpieces. Boucher, Cochin, and Eisen provided designs for the remaining plates. Vol. 1: engraved frontispiece, engraved title page, 24 engraved headpieces, 18 engraved tailpieces, 22 engraved plates; vol. 2: engraved title page, 22 engraved headpieces, 19 engraved tailpieces, 22 engraved plates; vol. 3: engraved title page, 22 engraved headpieces, 19 engraved tailpieces, 22 engraved plates; vol. 4: engraved title page, 22 engraved headpieces, 20 engraved tailpieces, 22 engraved plates; vol. 5: engraved title page, 22 engraved headpieces, 22 engraved tailpieces, 22 engraved plates. See Ray 15 for a list of the engravers.

REFERENCES: Cohen-de Ricci 158-160; Ray 15.

The Decameron, a collection of one hundred short stories told over ten days by ten wealthy young men and women, was written in 1349-1350 by the great humanist and poet Giovanni Boccaccio (1313-1375). These *novelle*, often humorous, are told in a lively fashion to distract the young people who are vacationing away from the city in order to escape the plague. While many of the stories have lofty themes, the humorous love stories have always been among the most popular and surely accounted for the tremendous popularity of *The Decameron* in the eighteenth century. Several of the lighter stories were recast by La Fontaine and included in his *Contes et nouvelles en vers* (see cat. no. 19).

This edition of *The Decameron*, with its large number of plates and tailpieces, was extremely popular. In addition to the Italian language edition exhibited here, the publishers issued a French translation with the same illustrations between 1757 and 1761. There were also editions dated 1779 and 1791 which contained reduced copies of the plates found in the 1757 edition. The credit for its success goes to Hubert François Bourguignon, known as Gravelot (1699-1773), for it is his lively designs which so perfectly complement the text. Of the other designers, only Boucher measures up to the high standard set by Gravelot.

By reading carefully and selecting just the right moment, Gravelot captured the essence of each story. He is at home depicting both the wealthy and the poor and in creating convincing settings of all kinds. In the plate illustrating the fifth story of the ninth day (vol. 5, facing p. 35), Gravelot has provided a highly detailed hayloft containing sheaves, tools, and sacks of grain. The artist selected the tale's climax when the poor fellow, Calandrino, is caught by his wife as he attempts to seduce Niccolosa. Calandrino's friends, partially hidden off to the left, had actually arranged for Calandrino's wife to arrive in time to catch him. The wife's anger, Calandrino's helplessness (Niccolosa was in on the trick), and the pranksters' delight are all captured in an illustration measuring less than 2½ x 4 inches. In plate after plate, and in the tailpieces as well, Gravelot captures both the details and the sense of Boccaccio's lively tales.

J.D.W.

H. Gravelot inv.   L V N. 7.   Ouvrier Sculp.

18. JEAN BAPTISTE RACINE

Oeuvres de Racine. Paris: 1760.
3 vols. Vol. 1: [4], xviii, [6], 414 p.,
[6] leaves of plates; vol. 2: [4], iv,
447 p., [5] leaves of plates; vol. 3:
[4], iv, 412 p., [2] leaves of plates.
Page size: 11¼ x 8⁵⁄₁₆ in.
(286 x 211 mm.) Binding: Full brown
calf gilt. Robert Sterling Clark
Collection.

ILLUSTRATIONS: Jacques de Sève
designed all the illustrations. Vol. 1:
engraved frontispiece, engraved title-
page vignette, 5 engraved plates,
5 engraved headpieces, 19 engraved
tailpieces; vol. 2: engraved title-page
vignette, 5 engraved plates, 5 engraved headpieces, 22 engraved tailpieces; vol. 3: engraved title-page
vignette, 2 engraved plates, 3 engraved headpieces, 19 engraved tailpieces. Most of the engraving was
carried out by Flipart and Baquoy,
but for a complete list of the engravers
see Ray 60.

REFERENCES: Cohen-de Ricci 846-
847; Ray 60.

Racine (1639-1699), known for his classical style, wrote twelve plays between 1664 and 1691. All of these, as well as minor essays and poems, are included in this edition of his works. While collections of Racine's writings had been published previously, this edition of 1760 was the first to be published on such a large scale and with such a wealth of illustration.

By employing a single artist, Jacques de Sève (act. 1742-1788), to design all the illustrations, from the full-page illustrations to the small tailpieces, the publisher insured a high degree of stylistic unity. This unity was frequently lacking when multiple artists and engravers worked on the same publication, a practice common in the eighteenth and nineteenth centuries. Yet uniformity could still be achieved if the designers and/or the engravers assumed a common style (see cat. nos. 20-22). And since de Sève's designs for many of the smaller images are not merely decorative devices but are miniature scenes whose subjects relate to the play being illustrated, the publication achieves a marvelous coherence of subject matter as well as style.

For the beautiful plate, engraved by Flipart, illustrating the play *Mithridate* (vol. 2, facing p. 185), de Sève chose the climactic moment in the drama. A messenger, sent by the aged King Mithridates to Monime, the beautiful young woman he had intended to marry and has already made queen, prevents her from drinking the poison the king, just minutes earlier, had commanded her to take. In the background we see King Mithridates, having fallen on his own sword to avoid capture by the invading Romans, being carried by his faithful son, Xiphares, to Monime's chamber where the king, with his dying breath, blesses the union of Monime and Xiphares whom he knows to be in love. De Sève has skillfully coalesced the haste of the messenger, Monime's heroic resolve, and her attendants' anxiety into a highly compelling figure group. Both the distant action and the foreground drama unfold within an architectural setting which is scaled to monumentalize the scene. De Sève's style, with its strong undercurrent of Baroque clarity and monumentality, is perfectly suited to Racine's classical dramas.

J.D.W.

MITHRIDATE.

19. JEAN DE LA FONTAINE

Contes et nouvelles en vers. . . .
Amsterdam [i.e., Paris: Barbou],
1762. 2 vols. Vol. 1: xiv, [2],
268, [2], 8 p., [40] leaves of plates;
vol. 2: [2], viii, [2], 306, [3],
[9]-16 [i.e., 8] p., [42] leaves of
plates. Page size: 7⅛ x 4½ in.
(182 x 114 mm.) Binding: Full red
morocco gilt, by Derome le jeune.
Robert Sterling Clark Collection.

ILLUSTRATIONS: Vol. 1: frontispiece
engraved by Ficquet after Rigaud;
title-page vignette, full-page vignette, headpiece, and 23 tailpieces
designed and engraved by Choffard;
39 engraved plates after Eisen. Vol. 2:
frontispiece engraved by Ficquet after
Vispré; title-page vignette, full-page
vignette, headpiece, and 29 tailpieces
designed and engraved by Choffard;
41 plates engraved after Eisen. See
Ray 26 for a list of the engravers.

REFERENCES: Cohen-de Ricci 558-
571; Ray 26.

NOTES:
1. Since the Middle Ages, a *fermier
général* was given a contract, by the
crown, to collect certain kinds of taxes
for the government. It was a very
lucrative business, and in the
eighteenth century financiers bought
these contracts for huge amounts.

This collection of La Fontaine's delightful, and often risqué, verse tales based upon Boccaccio, Ariosto, Machiavelli, and others had been published originally in the 1660s and 1670s. Perfectly suited to the tastes of the French upper classes in the eighteenth century, the *Contes* appeared in a number of editions from the 1740s to the 1780s. This edition was greatly admired at the time, for there were at least five other editions with copies of these illustrations published within fifteen years of its appearance in 1762.

Charles Eisen's (1720-1788) designs for the plates and Pierre Philippe Choffard's (1730-1809) tailpieces are filled with a vitality, freshness, and humor which exactly match La Fontaine's verses. Commissioned by an association of financiers called the *Fermiers Généraux*,[1] this publication was surely intended to demonstrate the "aristocratic" tastes of a group which had, by the middle of the eighteenth century, the wealth, but not the status, of the upper class. With their new money these tax-farmers created a publication that is, in some ways, the epitome of the Rococo: light, witty, elegant, sensual, decorative, and high in quality.

One can enjoy all these qualities in "Le Bât" ("The Pack-Saddle," vol. 2, p. 135, and the plate opposite). A jealous artist, having to leave home, paints a donkey on his wife's navel as a kind of seal ("en guise de cachet"). While the husband is gone, a fellow artist who is in love with the wife comes to visit and, "God knows how," the donkey gets erased completely. Before departing the lover paints another donkey but, due to his faulty memory, puts a pack-saddle on the animal. When the husband comes home, the wife reveals the donkey as a witness of her fidelity. Enraged, the husband exclaims, "To hell with the witness and the one who saddled it." Eisen has set his scene in the husband's studio and placed the wife as if she were a model. But the lover, instead of painting on the nearby canvas, is about to decorate the woman's navel. Choffard's tailpiece, an attractive accompaniment to the printed page, combines artist's equipment, gar-lands, foliage, and the donkey (here with its pack-saddle) into an ensemble of trophies that complements both Eisen's plate and La Fontaine's little tale.

J.D.W.

LE BÂT.

Un peintre étoit, qui jaloux de sa femme,
Allant aux champs, lui peignit un baudet
Sur le nombril, en guise de cachet.
Un sien confrere amoureux de la Dame,
La va trouver, & l'âne efface net,
Dieu sçait comment ; puis un autre en remet,
Au même endroit, ainsi que l'on peut croire.
A celui-ci, par faute de mémoire,
Il mit un Bât ; l'autre n'en avoit point.
L'époux revient, veut s'éclaircir du point.
Voyez, mon fils, dit la bonne commere ;
L'âne est témoin de ma fidélité.
Diantre soit fait, dit l'époux en colere,
Et du témoin, & de qui l'a bâté.

20. OVID

Les métamorphoses d'Ovide, en
latin et en françois. . . . Paris: Guillyn,
1767-1771. 4 vols. Vol. 1: [4], xc,
264, [2] p., [50] leaves of plates;
vol. 2: viii, 355 p., [33] leaves of
plates; vol. 3: viii, 360 p., [37] leaves
of plates; vol. 4: viii, 367, 8 p., [22]
leaves of plates. Page size:
9⅞ x 7⅛ in. (251 x 181 mm.)
Binding: Full mottled calf gilt.
Robert Sterling Clark Collection.

ILLUSTRATIONS: Vol. 1: added title
page, 3-page dedication (on 2 leaves),
vignette on printed title page, and 6
headpieces designed and engraved by
Choffard; 47 plates engraved after
Boucher, Eisen, Gravelot, Le Prince,
Monnet, and Moreau. Vol. 2: vignette
on printed title page and 4 headpieces
designed and engraved by Choffard; 4
headpieces engraved by Choffard after
Monnet; 33 plates engraved after
Boucher, Eisen, Monnet, Moreau,
and Parizot. Vol. 3: vignette on
printed title page and 8 headpieces
designed and engraved by Choffard;
37 plates engraved after Boucher,
Eisen, Monnet, Moreau, and St.
Gois. Vol. 4: vignette on printed title
page, 8 headpieces, and a full-page
tailpiece engraved by Choffard; 22
plates engraved after Boucher, Eisen,
Monnet, and Moreau. See Ray 62 for
a list of the engravers of the plates.
This copy has the following characteristics which suggest the plates are
early impressions (see Ray 62): pl. 13
given to Eisen (later issues give it,
correctly, to Gravelot); pl. [135]
lettered "134" and pl. [138] lettered
"137" (in later impressions the numbers are corrected); pl. [28] lettered
"27" (not previously recorded).

REFERENCES: Cohen-de Ricci 769-
772; Ray 62.

NOTES:
1. For a general description of Ovid's
Metamorphoses, see cat. no. 5.

Just as Ovid's text includes most of the important subjects of classical
mythology,[1] this publication includes designs by three generations of
great French illustrators of the period. Present here are designs by two
artists born around 1700, François Boucher (1703-1770) and Gravelot
(see cat. no. 17), and plates designed by the young Moreau le jeune
(1741-1814), with the greatest number of plates designed by Charles Eisen,
who was fifty years old in 1770. In addition, the headpieces, title-page
vignettes, and the impressive full-page tailpiece at the end of the fourth
volume are by Choffard, the most prolific and imaginative engraver of such
decorative elements (see cat. no. 19).

Despite the large number of designers and engravers, these volumes
exhibit less diversity than might be suspected. This is achieved, in part,
because the reproductive engravers shared a set of conventions which gives
all the plates a similar "look." In addition, the high level of quality
throughout is the result of the publishers matching the diverse subjects to
the styles and conceptions of the various artists. So while Eisen, whose
designs were well known for their grace and elegant charm, was responsible
for the illustrations of the four seasons, such scenes as Diana bathing were
given to Boucher, the artist best known for his voluptuous nudes.

In "Diana and Actaeon" Ovid describes the luscious coolness of the
spot where Diana and her nymphs are bathing when Actaeon, by chance,
intrudes. Diana blushes and splashes water on him, but, because he has
seen chaste Diana unclothed, Actaeon is punished by being turned into a
stag. His own hounds then pursue and kill him. For his design (vol. 1, pl. 41,
facing p. 201), Boucher created a marvelous foreground of nude figures.
Diana's gesture (the goddess can be identified by the crescent moon over her
brow) connects this lighter foreground with the shadowed distance where
we see Actaeon just beginning to sprout horns. The glances of the nymphs,
Diana's gesture, and the drapery overhead activate the composition, while
the engraver, St.-Aubin, causes the light to flicker over the surface. This
dynamic quality, so typical of the period, may be contrasted with a more
staid and controlled sixteenth-century woodcut illustration of the subject
(see cat. no. 5).

J.D.W.

F. Boucher del.   Aug. de St Aubin Sculp.

Diane se baignant avec ses Nymphes est
apperçue par Actéon, qu'elle Métamorphose
aussitot en Cerf.

21. JEAN BENJAMIN DE LA BORDE

Choix de chansons, mises en musique par M. de La Borde . . . ornées d'estampes par J. M. Moreau. . . . Paris: de Lormel, 1773. 4 vols., engraved throughout. Vol. 1: 154, [3] p.; vol. 2: 153 p., [1] leaf of plates; vol. 3: 150, [3] p., [1] leaf of plates; vol. 4: 150, [3] p., [1] leaf of plates. Bound in: 3 p. of verses in manuscript attributed to La Borde. Page size: 9⅞ x 6⁷⁄₁₆ in. (251 x 163 mm.) Binding: Full marbled calf gilt. Bookplate of Dumoulin du Lys. Robert Sterling Clark Collection.

ILLUSTRATIONS: Vol. 1: portrait of La Borde engraved by Moreau after Denon[1] tipped in on a binder's blank leaf, title-page vignette designed and engraved by Moreau, dedication engraved by Masquelier after Moreau, 25 full-page illustrations designed and engraved by Moreau;[2] vol. 2: engraved title page after Le Bouteux, 25 engraved full-page illustrations after Le Bouteux; vol. 3: engraved title page after Le Barbier, 25 engraved full-page illustrations after Le Barbier; vol. 4: engraved title page after Le Barbier, 19 engraved full-page illustrations after Le Barbier, 6 engraved full-page illustrations after Saint-Quentin. Title pages and plates in vols. 2-4 engraved by Masquilier and Née.

REFERENCES: Cohen-de Ricci 534-538; Ray 49.

NOTES:

1. No. 21, third state in Emmanuel Bocher, *Les gravures françaises du XVIIIᵉ siècle . . . Jean-Michel Moreau le jeune* (Paris: Damascène Morgand et Charles Fatout, 1882).

2. Ibid., nos. 862, 863, and 864-888.

3. Ray 49.

Idealized rural settings, handsome youths courting lovely young women, and simple pleasures—these subjects occur frequently in the songs published in these four volumes. It is not, however, a collection of popular songs to be sung by country folk, but rather a collection of poems by a number of people set to music by La Borde (1734-1794), a favorite of Louis XV and a *fermier général* (see cat. no. 19). La Borde, with the financial assistance of the king, arranged for their publication. As Ray says, "Its 100 plates and engraved text carry vanity publication to its furthest reach."[3] The pastoral themes, so prevalent in this collection, are a form of nostalgia intended for a highly refined and urbane public.

For Jean Michel Moreau le jeune (1741-1814, called "the younger" because he had an older brother who was also an artist), the twenty-five plates in volume 1 represent the first of several major commissions. Throughout the 1770s and 1780s Moreau was the most sought-after illustrator in Paris. He had participated in earlier publications (see cat. no. 20) and would soon begin the designs for his greatest achievement (see cat. no. 22), but for La Borde's music he not only provided the designs but also engraved the plates. This was seldom the case in French eighteenth-century illustration (Choffard's brilliant work with headpieces and tailpieces is an important exception, see cat. nos. 19 and 20), and it is rare in Moreau's oeuvre as well. Given the impressive results in the first volume of *Choix de chansons*, it is a pity that a falling-out between Moreau and La Borde led to the employment of other illustrators for volumes 2-4.

In his illustration (p. 12) to "Les amours de Glicere et d'Alexis," Moreau places the pleading Alexis and the coy Glicere in an idyllic setting which strongly suggests the happy outcome of this simple romance. The doves above, the hen and chicks in the foreground, and the grapevine clinging to the cottage give substance to the contentment and rural harmony found in so many of the songs in the four volumes. In addition, the oblique view of the cottage, the extreme shift from foreground to background, and the surface of flickering lights and darks vitalize this pastoral theme. Without Moreau's masterful illustrations, La Borde's publication would surely have been long forgotten.

J.D.W.

Ah! dit-il, un seul moment,
Ecoutés votre Amant.

J.M. moreau le j.me inv. sculp. 1772.

22. AUTHOR UNKNOWN

Suite d'estampes pour servir à l'histoire des moeurs et du costume des françois dans le dix-huitième siècle: année 1774. Paris: Imprimerie de Prault, 1784; [—*Seconde suite . . . année 1776*. Paris, 1777; *Troisieme suite . . . année 1783*. Paris, 1783]. [14] *l.*, [12] leaves of plates; [15] *l.*, [12] leaves of plates; [13] *l.*, [12] leaves of plates. Page size: 20⁹⁄₁₆ x 14¹³⁄₁₆ in. (521 x 376 mm.) Binding: Full marbled calf gilt. Robert Sterling Clark Collection.

ILLUSTRATIONS: In the first suite, 12 engraved plates after Freudeberg; in the second suite, 12 engraved plates after Moreau; in the third suite, 12 engraved plates after Moreau. The plates in the second and third suites are all in the next-to-last state except for pl. 16 which, lacking the number, is in the third state.[1] See Cohen-de Ricci 353-355 for a list of the titles and engravers.

REFERENCES: Cohen-de Ricci 352-362.[2]

NOTES:

1. For a description of the states of each plate by Moreau, see Emmanuel Bocher, *Les gravures françaises du XVIIIᵉ siècle . . . Jean-Michel Moreau le jeune* (Paris: Damascène Morgand et Charles Fatout, 1882), nos. 1348-1371.

2. In the Clark copy the first suite is a later edition.

3. This publication is described in Ray 55.

4. The first suite depicts a day in the life of a young woman of fashion; in the second she discovers her pregnancy, gives birth to a son, and resumes her life in society; the third describes the day of a young gallant.

The volume exhibited here contains the three suites in their rarest form, for seldom are they found with the text with which they were originally published. (The first suite, although it has the original descriptive text, is a later edition; it first appeared in 1775.) Moreau le jeune's illustrations are better known in the 1789 publication entitled *Monument du costume* which omitted the plates from the first suite but reprinted the twenty-four plates (in a later state) designed by Moreau, included two plates after Freudeberg not included in the first suite, and provided a text by Restif de la Bretonne.[3] The inclusion of the first suite in the Clark volume allows one to appreciate the scope of the project as originally conceived.

Among the plates in these impressive suites may be found some of the greatest costume prints ever published. Their significance derives, in part, from the high quality of the plates—some of those by Moreau are considered to be his best work. In addition, the illustrations, unlike most collections of fashion plates, form three narrative sequences which greatly enliven the series.[4] Finally, the work is of great significance because it documents activities, manners, and the decorative arts as well as fashion. Thanks to the ingenuity of Jean Henri Eberts, the Swiss banker who conceived of and "produced" these suites, we have thirty-six large-scale prints which describe, in greater detail than any text, both the manners and the material environment of the fashionable upper class in France on the eve of the French Revolution.

As can be seen in *Les adieux*, plate 22, Moreau's brilliant design and the engraver's expert translation onto copper admirably fulfilled Eberts's intentions. In the straightforward text Cephise goes to the opera with her husband and another relative; for the illustration Moreau created a psychologically complex drama. Cephise, in her spectacular gown, turns to acknowledge the relative's gallant gesture while her husband, already in the opera box, has turned his attention to the stage. Despite their differing moods and emotions, the figures move within a single arc with the grace of dancers. Details of costume, architecture, glance, and gesture are held within the broad contrasts of light and dark. As in many of the illustrations in the second and third suites, Moreau's brilliant design turns the fashion plate into great art.

J.D.W.

Désiné par J. M. Moreau le jeune.

en Gravé par de Launay le jeune en 1777.

Les adieux.

A.P.D.R.

Nº 22.

23. JEAN CLAUDE RICHARD DE SAINT-NON

Voyage pittoresque, ou Description des royaumes de Naples et de Sicile. . . . Paris: 1781-1786.
4 vols. in 5. Vol. 1: [4], xiii, [3], 252 p., [50] leaves of plates (3 folded); vol. 2: [4], xxiii, 283, [1] p., [83] leaves of plates (1 folded); vol. 3: [4], 6, [2], iv, xl, 201 p., [64] leaves of plates (4 folded); vol. 4, first part: [4], ii, xviii, [4], 266 p., [71] leaves of plates (1 folded); vol. 4, second part: [4], iv, [2], [267]-429, [1] p., [36] leaves of plates. Page size: 19¾ x 12⅞ in. (502 x 327 mm.) Binding: Full marbled calf gilt. Bookplate of W. R. Juynboll. Purchase 1964.

ILLUSTRATIONS: 5 engraved title-page vignettes, 2-page engraved dedication, 15 engraved headpieces, 96 engraved tailpieces, 304 leaves of engraved plates.[1] Choffard, Fragonard, Robert, Paris, and Saint-Non are among those who provided designs. For a complete list of the designers and engravers of the illustrations see Cohen-de Ricci 929.

REFERENCES: Brunet V, 55-56; Cohen-de Ricci 928-930; Ray 34.

NOTES:
1. The Clark copy includes the 14 extra plates called the "double medals" but lacks the plate showing an ancient sculpture of a phallus mentioned in Cohen-de Ricci 929 and Brunet V, 55.
2. For a recent discussion of Saint-Non's participation in the publication, see Antony Griffiths, "The Contract between Laborde and Saint-Non for the *Voyage pittoresque de Naples et de Sicile*," *Print Quarterly* 5 (1988): 408-414.

Saint-Non (1727-1791) was not, in fact, the major author of this famous travel book. The text is by a number of individuals, including Saint-Non; but since he was the financial backer and prime mover of the project, he is generally credited with its authorship.[2] The work was a tremendous undertaking of time and money. Issued initially in installments beginning in 1778, the publication took almost eight years to complete, utilized the drawings of fourteen artists, and required forty-three engravers. A great deal of Saint-Non's considerable wealth and some of his brother's was invested in the project. With unflagging energy, an admirable concern for accuracy, and a single-minded devotion to quality, Saint-Non created one of the great monuments of travel literature and illustration.

Concentrating on Sicily and the region of Naples, the *Voyage pittoresque* provides extensive visual and documentary information on cities, architecture, and trade as well as social and religious customs from ancient times up to the date of publication. The first of a pair of plates depicts a temple at Pompeii as it appeared at the time; the other shows the same temple as it might have looked in the first century A.D., complete with a religious ceremony in progress. Many of the plates present views of towns and the surrounding countryside, but there is also a section illustrating Renaissance paintings in Naples and another which shows Vesuvius in eruption. With a scholarly text and with illustrations commissioned from a number of artists over three decades (some of the illustrations are based on drawings made for Saint-Non by Jean Honoré Fragonard and Hubert Robert in the early 1760s), Saint-Non conveyed, with great thoroughness, the history and variety to be found in southern Italy.

Perhaps it is the richness of the archaeological remains which has most captivated readers of the *Voyage pittoresque*. In many plates the ruins of Greek and Roman temples evoke a romantic fascination with great monuments in decay. In the marvelous image of a temple at Paestum (vol. 3, facing p. 157), Hubert Robert (1733-1808) captures a mood as well as the facts associated with the site. We can clearly see the design of the building and we know its scale by comparing the figures with the architectural fragments on which they lean; but by juxtaposing the jagged tree at the left (surely an invention of the artist) with the massive stone structure, Robert invites meditation on the forces in nature and the downfall of civilizations.

J.D.W.

Vue du Temple Exastile Periptere de Pattum près de Salernes à 20. lieues de Naples.

Dessiné d'après nature par M.ᵉ Robert Peintre du Roi

A General History of Quadrupeds, the figures engraved on wood by T. Bewick. Newcastle upon Tyne: S. Hodgson, R. Beilby, & T. Bewick, 2nd ed., 1791. x, 483 p. Page size: 8⅞ x 5⅝ in. (226 x 143 mm.) Binding: Full brown morocco gilt, by the Club Bindery, 1900. Bookplate of Robert Hoe. Robert Sterling Clark Collection.

ILLUSTRATIONS: 275 illustrations of quadrupeds and pictorial tailpieces wood-engraved by Bewick.

REFERENCES: Roscoe 2b, variant B.

NOTES:

1. Bewick was able to create these minute details and subtle shifts from light to dark by using engraving tools on the hard, end grain of the block of wood. Such refinement was not typical of relief printing during the seventeenth and eighteenth centuries.

2. The *Quadrupeds*, first published in 1790, went through eight editions by 1828; both *Land Birds*, 1797, and *Water Birds*, 1804, went through eight.

3. Published in the 1826 edition of *Land Birds*, as quoted in Roscoe, p. xv.

4. Bewick, *A General History of Quadrupeds*, 334.

Thomas Bewick (1753-1828), by developing the technique of wood engraving, is rightly credited with reviving the use of relief printing for book illustration. Because images printed in relief, whereby the raised areas of the wood block or metal plate carry the ink, can be printed along with type which is similarly inked (see the illustration for cat. no. 15), they were generally employed for illustration until the seventeenth century (see cat. nos. 1-6). After 1600, and for the next two hundred years, engraving—one of several intaglio processes in which the ink is allowed to remain only in the lines incised on the plate—was favored for illustrations in most luxury publications because it could produce images that were thought to be of higher quality, more "refined," than was possible with relief cuts. Since intaglio illustrations and text must be printed separately, the cost of producing fine books during the seventeenth and eighteenth centuries was relatively high. By using relief cuts for the illustrations in his books, Bewick utilized the efficiencies of printing text and images together; and by creating detailed and extremely sensitive images, he demonstrated that the "lowly" relief print could provide great illustrations.[1]

Bewick's books on animals were widely read during his lifetime.[2] Their popularity was the result, in large measure, of his success in appealing to a broad spectrum, especially children, by combining education and entertainment. Near the end of his life, the artist described this dual function:

My writings were intended chiefly for youth . . . and the more readily to allure their . . . attention . . . I illustrated them by figures delineated with all the fidelity and animation I was able to impart . . . and as instruction is of little avail without constant cheerfulness and occasional amusement, I interspersed the more serious studies with *Tale*-pieces of gaiety and humor; yet even in these seldom without an endeavor to illustrate some truth, or point some moral. . . .[3]

That Bewick was an inspired teacher is clearly evident in the vignettes illustrated on pages 336-337. For the marvelously detailed rendering of the hare on page 337, the illustrator stressed the animal's characteristic speed. On page 336 Bewick concludes the section on the dog with a fascinating tailpiece (or "tale"-piece, to use Bewick's pun) revealing this quadruped's "care in directing the steps of the blind man. . . ."[4] Buffeted by wind and rain, the poor fellow is utterly dependent on his dog as he shuffles across the dilapidated bridge. In an image barely 2 x 3¼ inches, Bewick, a sensitive and compassionate observer of his fellow man, describes both the precariousness of the blind man's situation and the heroic task given to the little dog.

J.D.W.

before him on a journey, often going over the same
ground; on coming to crofs ways, ftops, looks back, and
waits to obferve which of them he takes; fits up and
begs; and, when it has committed a theft, flinks away,
with its tail between its legs; is an enemy to beggars
and ill-looking people, and attacks them without the leaft
provocation; is alfo faid to be fick at the approach of bad
weather.——We cannot, however, agree with the learned
naturalift, when he afferts, that the male puppies refem-
ble the Dog, and the female the Bitch; or that it is a
character common to the whole fpecies, that the tail always bends to the left fide. To thefe we may add, as
equally void of foundation, a remark of M. Buffon, that
a female Hound, covered with a Dog of her own kind,
has been known to produce a mixed race, confifting of
Hounds and Terriers.——We barely mention thefe, to
fhew, that too much caution cannot be ufed in forming
general characters or fyftematic arrangements; and we
leave it to the experience of the moft inattentive obferver
to detect fuch palpable abfurdities.

The HARE.

THIS harmlefs and inoffenfive animal, deftitute of
every means of defence, and furrounded on all
fides by its enemies, would foon be utterly extirpated,
if Nature, ever kind and provident, had not endowed it
with faculties, by which it is frequently enabled to evade
their purfuit.

Fearful of every danger, and attentive to every alarm,
the Hare is continually upon the watch; and being provided with very long ears, moveable at pleafure, and
eafily directed to every quarter, is warned of the moft
diftant approaches of danger. Its eyes are large and prominent, adapted to receive the rays of light on every fide,
and give notice of more immediate alarms. To thefe
may be added its great fwiftnefs, by which it foon leaves
moft of its purfuers far behind.——The hind are much
longer than the fore legs, and are furnifhed with ftrong
mufcles, which give the Hare a fingular advantage in
running up a hill; and, as if fenfible of its powers in
this refpect, it is always obferved to fly towards rifing
ground when firft ftarted.

Y

25. PIERRE JOSEPH BERNARD

Oeuvres de P. J. Bernard, ornées de gravures d'après les dessins de Prud'hon; la dernière estampe gravée par lui-même. Paris: P. Didot l'aîné, 1797, an V. [4], xi, [1], 300 p., [8] leaves of plates. One of 150 copies printed on "papier-vélin fort d'Angoulême." Page size: 12⅝ x 9½ in. (321 x 241 mm.) Binding: ½ red morocco gilt, by Champs. Robert Sterling Clark Collection.

ILLUSTRATIONS: Each of the 4 designs by Prud'hon in 2 states, for a total of 8 plates. The first two designs, engraved by Beisson, appear in the first and second states. The third design, engraved by Copia, appears in the third and fifth states, as does the fourth design, engraved by Prud'hon.[1]

REFERENCES: Cohen-de Ricci 133-134.

NOTES:

1. There are two catalogues raisonnés of the work of Prud'hon. The most recent is Jean Guiffrey, *L'oeuvre de Pierre-Paul Prud'hon*, Archives de l'art français, nouv. pér., t. 13 (Paris: Librairie Arman Colin, 1924). For a more thorough treatment of the various states of the plates, see Edmond de Goncourt, *Catalogue raisonné de l'oeuvre peint, dessiné et gravé de P. P. Prud'hon* (Paris: Rapilly, 1876), cat. nos. 4, 129-131.

2. As published in Emile Dacier, "Prud'hon et l'art du livre," *Le Portique*, 2 (1945): 68-82.

3. Carol Margot Osborne, "Pierre Didot the Elder and French book illustration" (Ph.D. diss., Stanford University, 1979), 64-65. This study also includes a useful "Catalogue of illustrated classics published by Pierre Didot," 182-257.

Pierre Didot l'aîné (1761-1853) was the leading publisher of illustrated books in Revolutionary France. Utilizing the roman typeface designed by his brother Firmin Didot and commissioning illustrations under the artistic direction of Jacques Louis David, Didot published the classics of French literature in lavish editions which are monuments of the Neoclassical style. Artists closely associated with these editions include Girodet, Gérard, and Chaudet.

The artistic style of Pierre Paul Prud'hon (1758-1832) is not entirely within the Neoclassical tradition. And while Prud'hon never received the approval of David, he did receive some commissions, as Pierre Didot himself was a great admirer. Didot made this clear when he published this edition of Bernard's *Oeuvres*, which includes Didot's dedicatory verse, "Epitre à mon ami Prud'hon . . . ," which ends with the words "Oui, cher Prud'hon, ce seul ouvrage t'assure l'immortalité."

Pierre Joseph Bernard (1710-1775) was known as "Gentil-Bernard," which was how Voltaire referred to him in a letter urging him to complete "L'art d'aimer," the first poem in this collection of his work. "L'art d'aimer," an erotic poem written in an Ovidian manner, provided the inspiration for Prud'hon's first three illustrations. The fourth plate, shown here, accompanies the poem "Phrosine et Mélidor," a story of the separation and reunification of two lovers.

Prud'hon's moonlit scene of the reunited lovers is mysterious and haunting; the image remains with the reader long after the poem has been forgotten. It also has the distinction of being the only engraving ever executed by the artist himself. Delacroix was so impressed that he exclaimed that its creation would suffice to place Prud'hon next to Correggio.[2]

The Clark copy of this work exemplifies a typical deluxe edition produced by Pierre Didot. It was customary for Didot to issue a limited number of copies with the unlettered states of the plates and occasionally an even more limited number of copies with the etched states of the plates.[3] Collectors were most interested, however, in copies which contained the plates in two or more of the various states. The Clark copy contains each of the four plates in both the lettered and unlettered states.

S.R.

26. MUSAEUS

Héro et Léandre; poëme nouveau en trois chants, traduit du grec, sur un manuscrit trouve a Castro, auquel on a joint des notes historiques. Cette édition est ornée d'un frontispiece et de huit estampes en couleur, dessinées et gravées par P. L. Debucourt, de la ci-devant académie. Paris: Imprimerie de Pierre Didot l'aîné, an IX, 1801. 100, [1] p., [9] leaves of plates. Page size: 12¾ x 10 in. (327 x 253 mm.) Binding: ½ olive morocco gilt, by Canape. Robert Sterling Clark Collection.

ILLUSTRATIONS: Black and white aquatint frontispiece and 8 engraved color plates by Debucourt; all 9 plates appear in the final state.[1]

REFERENCES: Cohen-de Ricci 833-834; Ray 88.

NOTES:

1. For a detailed description of the various states of the plates, see Maurice Fenaille, *L'oeuvre gravé par P.-L. Debucourt, 1755-1832* (Paris: Librairie Damascène Morgand, 1899), cat. nos. 123-131.

2. Albert Vauflart and Jacques Herrold enumerate these techniques in an essay, "Les procédés de gravures," *Exposition Debucourt* (Paris: Société pour l'étude de la gravure française, 1920), 65-82.

Little is known of the Greek poet Musaeus who wrote of Hero and Leander in the 4th or 5th century A.D. But the legend, in which Leander of Abydos drowns while crossing the Hellespont to his lover Hero, the priestess of Aphrodite at Sestos, has survived in various manifestations. The story inspired Marlowe's *Hero and Leander* (1598) and Lord Byron's *The Bride of Abydos*, published in 1813, a few years after Byron himself swam from Abydos to Sestos.

This is another production of Pierre Didot (see cat. no. 25), who in this case employed the talents of the greatest color printer of the era to illustrate this translation of the legend by Le Chevalier de Querelles. Philibert Louis Debucourt (1755-1832) was initially trained as a painter and, unlike other color printers of the period, always worked from his own drawings. He produced his first color prints in 1785 and over the next fifteen years experimented with at least ten different techniques, often employing many methods in a single print.[2] He is best known for the prints issued during these years, in particular for a lively series of engravings which depict the contemporary French social scene.

For *Héro et Léandre*, Debucourt chose to work in a more strictly Neoclassical mode that does not suit him particularly well. This is evident in the third plate, *La course*, in which the three runners with their hands extended are drawn as rigidly as the statue of Glory to their right, thus exhibiting little evidence of physical activity despite their race to the finish line. But the quality of the color is spectacular. For these illustrations Debucourt returned to an early, successful technique in which four successive plates were used to achieve the color, one for each of the primary colors and one for black.

S.R.

P. L. Debucourt

LA COURSE.

James Thomson (1700-1748) wrote "Winter" in 1725. Poems on the other three seasons appeared successively and the collected version of *The Seasons* was first published in 1730. These poems introduced a sympathetic appreciation of nature into the body of English literature which heretofore had been absent. Thomson's success was immediate and book illustrators in particular were quick to respond to his reverence towards nature. And they continued to respond throughout the eighteenth century. In France editions of *The Seasons* were illustrated by such accomplished artists as Eisen (Paris, 1759) and Le Barbier (Paris, 1795) and in England by the great master of wood engraving, Thomas Bewick (London, 1805).

But no English illustrations for *The Seasons* were as magnificent as those created by William Hamilton and engraved by Bartolozzi and Tomkins. These illustrations first appeared in a splendid folio edition published by Tomkins in 1797. The Clark copy is from 1807, when the work was printed in a quarto edition. The quarto edition does not contain the five tailpieces which appear in the 1797 edition and is certainly not as grand, but the illustrations are otherwise identical.

William Hamilton (1751-1801) was primarily a history painter who drew his inspiration from literature. He illustrated editions of Shakespeare, Milton, and Gray, but the 1797 edition of *The Seasons* is his masterpiece. He successfully captured the pastoral sentiment expressed by Thomson in such scenes as this countryman fishing, the title vignette for "Summer," in which the landscape is depicted with picturesque detail and man's place therein is harmonious.

The engraving of these illustrations was executed by the leading stipple engraver in England, Francesco Bartolozzi (1724-1815), and his most accomplished student, Peltro William Tomkins (1760-1840), who also published the folio edition of 1797. Bartolozzi and Tomkins excelled in producing color prints *à la poupée* from their stipple-engraved plates, a method in which the colors are painted onto a single plate. Yet they produced only a few copies of *The Seasons* with the plates printed in color.

S.R.

SUMMER.

28. JOHANN WOLFGANG
    VON GOETHE

Faust, tragédie de M. de Goethe, traduite en français par M. Albert Stapfer. . . . Paris: Ch. Motte & Sautelet, 1828. [4], iv, 148 p., [18] leaves of plates. Page size: 16¹⁵⁄₁₆ x 11⅜ in. (430 x 289 mm.) Binding: Full black morocco gilt, by Noulhac. Purchase 1989.

ILLUSTRATIONS: Lithographed frontispiece and 17 lithographed plates in the first published state on *chine collé* by Eugène Delacroix.[1] Two versions of the original lithographed wrappers by Achille Devéria and a pen and ink drawing by Charles Henri Pille are bound in.

REFERENCES: Carteret 270-272; Ray 143.

NOTES:

1. For a detailed description of the states of each of the plates, see Loys Delteil, *Le peintre-graveur illustré (XIXᵉ et XXᵉ siècles)*, vol. 3, *Ingres & Delacroix* (1908; reprint, New York: Collectors Editions Ltd. and Da Capo Press, 1968), cat. nos. 57-74.

Goethe (1749-1832) has filled his drama with strong emotions, violent actions, and strange images, while darkness and mystery are the keynotes of this great example of Romanticism. Mephistopheles, the devil who guides Faust, gains entrance to the scholar's study disguised as a poodle, surprises some carousing students by turning wine into fire, and takes Faust to a witches' sabbath full of monstrous apparitions. Faust kills a man in a duel and Marguerite, whom Faust has seduced, becomes insane with guilt and kills her newborn child. Underscoring human weakness in the face of the powers of evil, Goethe's drama presents a multitude of experiences and emotions well outside the rational.

Eugène Delacroix (1798-1863) had mastered the lithographic medium by the time he provided the illustrations to *Faust*. Such processes as engraving or etching on metal and cutting or engraving on wood require a technical skill most artists left to craftsmen using specialized tools. Lithography, on the other hand, allowed the creative artist to draw directly onto the printing surface or onto paper that permitted the image to be transferred directly onto the lithographic stone or plate. Delacroix recognized the medium's potential for retaining a design's spontaneity and freedom, qualities often diminished when the artist's design was translated by the reproductive engraver onto copper or wood. In the plate shown here (opposite p. 38), which depicts Mephistopheles' sudden appearance before a seated Faust, the rapid marks and loosely defined forms are reproduced exactly the way they were drawn. Also visible, in Faust's robe for example, are the white lines where Delacroix scraped through the black already put down. Delacroix's style—full of energy, immediacy, and vitality—is perfectly suited to lithography, while his tendency toward the dramatic and the emotional is perfectly suited to Goethe's *Faust*.

The Clark copy is of particular interest for a number of reasons. The prints, on very smooth, thin paper fixed to heavier paper, a technique called *chine collé*, are wonderfully strong and fresh. The binding is impressive with its rich colors and complex gilding. Bound in are the wrappers in which the book was originally issued and which carry lithographed designs by another Romantic artist, Achille Devéria (1800-1857). And, finally, a fully developed drawing of Faust in his study by the illustrator Charles Henri Pille (1844-1897) is also bound in. There is a sumptuousness about this object which is in keeping with the book's outstanding significance.

J.D.W.

Meph : Pourquoi tout ce vacarme ? que demande Monsieur ? qu'y a t il pour son service ?

29. JOSEPH ADOLPHE
FERDINAND LANGLÉ

Les contes du gay sçavoir; bal-
lades, fabliaux et traditions du moyen
âge, publiés par Ferd. Langlé, et
ornés de vignettes et fleurons, imités
des manuscrits originaux par
Bonington et Monnier. [Paris]: Firmin
Didot, pour Lami Denozan, Libraire,
1828. [6], cxlvi, 48 p., [1] leaf of
plates. Page size: 8½ x 5⅜ in.
(215 x 137 mm.) Binding: Full red
morocco gilt, by Muller. Bookplate of
Jacques Vieillard. Robert Sterling
Clark Collection.

ILLUSTRATIONS: Lithographed title
page, 10 lithographed headpieces
printed on *chine collé*, and 15 wood-
engraved decorated initials, all hand
colored. The title page is by
Bonington and the vignettes are by
Bonington (6) and Monnier (4).

REFERENCES: Carteret 172-174;
Ray 114.

I t is difficult to know whether *Les contes du gay sçavoir* was intended as a literary hoax or as a playful satire on the prevailing fascination with medieval life. In any case, Ferdinand Langlé (1798-1867), a vaudeville actor and cousin of the Romantic novelist Eugène Sue, presented his curious collection of ballads and fables as if he were revealing newly discovered medieval material. The text is printed in gothic characters with illuminated initials, and there is a forty-eight page "Notes et Glossaire" appended at the end. However, there is no doubt that Langlé himself wrote these tales.

The illustrations by Henry Monnier (1799-1877) and Richard Parkes Bonington (1802-1828) are equally curious, for they are stylistically unlike the work for which either artist is known. Monnier is best known for his caricatures of the contemporary French middle class. Bonington, on the other hand, is famous for genre scenes and picturesque town and country views. But for *Les contes du gay sçavoir* each dabbled in the "Gothic trouba-dour" style of illustration, with imaginary renderings of the customs and costumes of the Middle Ages.

Monnier's illustrations are the least convincing; his crudely drawn figures have exaggerated facial expressions which reveal the satirical nature of the book. Bonington's illustrations are more gracefully executed, but they too are playful compositions in which a humorous intention is clear. This is especially true of his design for the title page. The composition of the page is accurate in its imitation of printed books of hours, but the jovial figures are suspicious, particularly in the vignette at the bottom of the page where one of the three putti is mounted on a hobbyhorse.

The Clark copy of this book is one of very few in which the title page, headpieces, and initials are all hand colored, as was originally intended.

S.R.

Les Contes du gay sçavoir.

Ballades, Fableaux et
traditions du moyen âge,
publiés par Ferd. Langlé,
et ornés de Vignettes et Fleurons,
imités des Manuscrits originaux
par Bonington et Monnier.
Imprimé par Firmin Didot,
pour Lami Denozan, Libraire,
rue des Fossés Montmartre, N.º 4.

la Damoiselle

l'Amoureux

M DCCXXVIII.

30. JEAN BAPTISTE
POQUELIN MOLIÈRE

Oeuvres de Molière, précédées
d'une notice sur sa vie et ses ouvrages
par M. Saint Beuve; vignettes par
Tony Johannot. Paris: Paulin, 1835-
1836. 2 vols. Vol. 1: 768, [1] p., [1]
leaf of plates; vol. 2: 895, [1] p. Page
size: 10½ x 7 in. (270 x 173 mm.)
Binding: ½ red calf, by Ysieux.
Purchase 1986.

ILLUSTRATIONS: Wood-engraved
frontispiece and 800 wood-engraved
vignettes, head- and tailpieces by
Porret, Thompson, Best, Lelior, and
others after Tony Johannot.

REFERENCES: Carteret 410-411;
Ray 181.

NOTES:

1. Molière, *Four Comedies*, trans. Richard
Wilbur (New York: Harcourt, Brace
Jovanovich, 1982), 418.

Molière (1622-1673) essentially created modern French comedy with such masterpieces as *Le Tartuffe* (1664) and *Le Misanthrope* (1666). Initially received with controversy, his comedies became enormously successful and remain so. The first illustrated edition of Molière's *Oeuvres* was published in 1682, with thirty-four plates after Pierre Brissart. Since then, countless editions have appeared, often illustrated by prominent artists. The eighteenth century produced two outstanding illustrated editions. The first, published in 1734, contained illustrations by Boucher and the second, issued in 1776, contained plates after Moreau le jeune.

In the nineteenth century, Tony Johannot (1803-1853) joined the ranks of Boucher and Moreau with this 1835-1836 edition of Molière's *Oeuvres* containing some eight hundred illustrations. Johannot was a prolific illustrator, with over 240 books to his credit. He was in great demand by leading Romantic novelists such as Eugène Sue and Victor Hugo, who wanted illustrations for their newest projects. But his artistic breadth was such that he did not hesitate to illustrate, in addition, religious works such as *Les saints évangiles* (Paris, 1836) and editions of the great French classics.

Johannot was also among the first French book illustrators to embrace the technique of wood engraving, which had been mastered by Thomas Bewick in England (see cat. no. 24). The technique had been introduced into France by Bewick's pupil Charles Thompson (1791-1843), who was one of the many artists who engraved Johannot's drawings for this edition of Molière's *Oeuvres*.

As wood engravings could be printed along with the text, Johannot was able to intersperse many images throughout the work, whereas his eighteenth-century predecessors, whose illustrations were printed separately, often found it necessary to depict a single scene in a given play. For example, Johannot created twenty-eight illustrations for *Le Tartuffe*, closely following the developments in each of the five acts. Molière's comedy, written in verse, revolves around the religious hypocrite Tartuffe, who wreaks havoc on the house of the enraptured Orgon. Under Tartuffe's influence, Orgon arranges the marriage of his daughter to the hypocrite, wills all of his property to him, and banishes his protesting son. Orgon is enlightened only when Tartuffe is caught seducing his wife, by which time his household can be saved only by the intervention of the king. Shown here is Johannot's depiction of Act 4, Scene 1, where Orgon's level-headed brother-in-law Cléante appeals to Tartuffe, asking "Would it not be the decent thing to beat a generous and honorable retreat?"[1]

S.R.

Souffrez, sans vous vouloir embarrasser de rien,
Qu'il soit à ses périls possesseur de son bien;
Et songez qu'il vaut mieux encor qu'il en mésuse
Que si de l'en frustrer il faut qu'on vous accuse.
J'admire seulement que, sans confusion,
Vous en ayez souffert la proposition.
Car enfin le vrai zèle a-t-il quelque maxime
Qui montre à dépouiller l'héritier légitime?
Et s'il faut que le ciel dans votre cœur ait mis
Un invincible obstacle à vivre avec Damis,
Ne vaudroit-il pas mieux qu'en personne discrète
Vous fissiez de céans une honnête retraite,
Que de souffrir ainsi, contre toute raison,
Qu'on en chasse pour vous le fils de la maison?
Croyez-moi, c'est donner de votre prud'hommie,
Monsieur...

TARTUFE. Il est, monsieur, trois heures et demie :

31. CHARLES JAMES APPERLEY

The Life of a Sportsman, by Nimrod. London: Rudolph Ackermann, Eclipse Sporting Gallery, 1842. vi, [2], 402 p., [36] leaves of plates, plus publisher's catalogue (10 p.) Page size: 9½ x 6 in. (242 x 150 mm.) Binding: Publisher's blue cloth gilt. Robert Sterling Clark Collection.

ILLUSTRATIONS: 36 aquatints by Alken, hand-colored, including frontispiece and added pictorial title page. Four are mounted on plate paper, one sheet of which is water-marked "1846."

REFERENCES: Mellon 167; Ray 1976, 46.

NOTES:

1. For a discussion of the development of English sporting art, see Stephen Deuchar, *Sporting Art in Eighteenth-Century England: A Social and Political History* (New Haven: Yale University Press, 1988).

The Life of a Sportsman by Charles James Apperley (1778-1843) is a preeminent example of the vogue in England for sporting books and pictures.[1] Better known by his pseudonym Nimrod, Apperley was a popular writer on hunting and racing and a sportsman *par excellence*, having devoted himself almost exclusively to fox-hunting between the years 1805 and 1820. To present a panorama of English sporting life, Nimrod tells a "half-true, half-fictitious" story of a country squire, beginning with his boyhood days when his sports were rat catching and rabbit and badger hunting. In his youth he was almost seduced by the attractions of the turf but, recognizing the moral superiority of "the higher sports of the field," contented himself with living on the ancestral acres as a "first-class fox-hunter, horseman, and coachman."

Looking at this classic sporting book we can understand why Henry Alken (1781-1851) was considered the premier sporting illustrator of his day. He captured the ebullient spirit of the narrative in a series of colored aquatint etchings. His style is clearly related to that of Thomas Rowlandson (1756-1822) and George Cruikshank (1792-1878), mingling deft caricature with a loving depiction of the English countryside.

By 1842 aquatint was no longer employed by most illustrators, but its ability to render tone and capture the clear washes of watercolor makes it a particularly attractive medium. Usually the plates were printed in one or two colors with the remaining colors added by hand. Rudolph Ackermann, the publisher of *The Life of a Sportsman*, had long been a great promoter of aquatint artists, and he issued many books and print series of a sporting and topographical nature featuring their works.

The fanciful title page of the Clark book faces a plate showing the gathering of the hunt in front of a large country seat. The overall high, bright color is tempered by lighter, almost autumnal tones of sky and ground. The title page exhibits a series of miniature vignettes enmeshed in a network of suitable sporting motifs which include crossed whips and spurs, a fox mask and brush with saddle, fishing rods and nets, guns, a stag head, and a racing trophy. The vignettes show a child playing at coaching, as well as scenes of racing, bird hunting, a typical after-the-hunt scene of jollification, coaching, driving, greyhound coursing, and fox-hunting. It is a part-playful, part-serious introduction to the text and a beautiful example of a hand-colored etching.

S.S.G.

THE
LIFE
OF A
SPORTSMAN
BY
NIMROD.

LONDON: PUBLISHED BY R. ACKERMANN, AT HIS ECLIPSE SPORTING GALLERY, 191 REGENT ST.   JULY 1842.

32. PAUL GAVARNI

Les lorettes. 1re série. [Paris: Aubert & cie.] En vente au Bureau du Charivari . . . et au Bureau du Journal pour rire, [1841-1843]. 79 leaves of plates, plus publisher's catalogue (15 p.). Original wrappers bound in. Page size: 13¼ x 10 in. (335 x 253 mm.) Binding: Contemporary purple cloth. Robert Sterling Clark Collection.

ILLUSTRATIONS: 79 hand-colored lithographed plates by Gavarni, printed by Aubert & cie. Plates 9, 21, 30, 33, 34, 42, 44, 46, 52, 53, 56-58, 61-74, 76, 77, 79 appear in the third state. The remainder appear in the second state, except plates 26 and 32, which appear in states after the legend, but not described by Armelhault and Bocher.[1]

REFERENCES: Beraldi VII, 51; Ray 155.

NOTES:

1. J. Armelhault and E. Bocher, *L'oeuvre de Gavarni; lithographies originales et essais d'eau-fort et de procédés nouveau: catalogue raisonné* (Paris: Librairies des bibliophiles, 1873), cat. nos. 763-841.

2. Therese Dolan Stamn, *Gavarni and the Critics* (Ann Arbor: UMI Research Press, 1981), 201 n. 13.

3. A recent study of the *grisette* and the *lorette* can be found in ibid., 125-158.

The lithographs of Guillaume Sulpice Chevallier, known as Paul Gavarni (1804-1866), appeared in numerous nineteenth-century journals. He began his own periodical, *Journal des gens du monde*, in 1833, but it failed after nineteen issues.[2] In 1837 he joined the staff of *Charivari*, where much of his work from the late 1830s and early 1840s was published and which became known for its keen observance and documentation of social types. Unlike his fellow caricaturists Henry Monnier and Honoré Daumier, who satirized the bourgeoisie, Gavarni preferred to observe the Parisian lower classes and, in particular, the lower-class courtesan.

The *lorette* was a particular type of courtesan unique to nineteenth-century Paris. Named for the neighborhood in which she lived, near the church *Notre Dame de Lorette*, she was not a prostitute, nor was she a kept woman. But she did enter into temporary liaisons with men for purely financial reward. Aspiring to wealth and a life of luxury, she relied on her graceful and elegant social charms to attract a suitable and prosperous lover. Yet she was cool and calculating in private.

Gavarni's seventy-nine lithographs depicting the *lorette* appeared in *Charivari* between 30 June 1841 and 30 December 1843. The biting legends which appear underneath each of the framed lithographs were also supplied by Gavarni. Shown here is an image which depicts two *lorettes* who have spotted their approaching lovers. One says, "Mine is blond . . . I hate blonds; you hate brunettes, so let's switch." The other replies, "You have no shame! Mine wears a dressing gown lined with silk throughout. I want to switch back. . . ."

In addition to the laconic *lorette*, Gavarni also observed the *grisette*, a courtesan of lower status, who entered into relationships with impoverished students, exchanging household chores and companionship for room and board.[3] The images of *grisettes* appeared in a series entitled *Les étudiants de Paris*, which appeared in *Charivari* from 1839 through 1842. Gavarni distinguished the class of these courtesans through his accurate designs for costumes and detailed analysis of social manner. It is interesting to note that in the early 1850s Gavarni again produced a series of lithographs devoted to the *lorette*. In *Les lorettes vieillies* (1852-1853), Gavarni portrays with equally keen observation the aging *lorette* whose only commodity, her beauty, is exhausted.

S.R.

Par Gavarni.

-Le mien est blond; ... j'aime pas les blonds; t'aime pas les bruns; changeons.
-T'es pas gênée! la robe de chambre du mien est doublée de satin partout. Je
veux du retour........

33. [Taxile Delord]

Un autre monde; transformations, visions, incarnations, ascensions, locomotions, explorations, pérégrinations, excursions, stations, cosmogonies, fantasmagories, rêveries, folateries, facéties, lubies, métamorphoses, zoomorphoses, lithomorphoses, métempsycoses, apothéoses et autres choses, par Grandville. Paris: H. Fournier, 1844. [4], 295, [1] p., [37] leaves of plates. Page size: 9¹³⁄₁₆ x 7⅛ in. (250 x 181 mm.) Binding: Publisher's ¼ red morocco gilt. Bookplate of Robert Nossam. Purchase 1989.

ILLUSTRATIONS: Frontispiece, 148 vignettes, and 36 hand-colored plates after Grandville, engraved on wood by various artists.

REFERENCES: Carteret 285; Ray 196.

NOTES:

1. Charles Baudelaire, *The Painter of Modern Life and Other Essays*, trans. and ed. Jonathon Mayne (London: Phaidon, 1964), 181.

2. Many authors enumerate the various influences of Grandville's *Un autre monde*. The most recent is Clive Getty, *Grandville, dessins originaux* (Nancy: Musée des beaux-arts, Cabinet des dessins, 1986), 340-347. For a more thorough treatment of Grandville's influence on Carroll, see Mario Praz, "Two Masters of the Absurd: Grandville and Carroll," *The Artist and the Book in France, Essays in Honor of Jean Seznec*, ed. Francis Haskell, Anthony Levi, and Robert Shackleton (Oxford: Clarendon Press, 1974), 134-137.

Un autre monde represents a major accomplishment in the history of illustrated books. For the first time, the images dictated the narrative, rather than vice versa. This intent is clearly indicated in the book's preface, which takes the form of a dialogue between "Le Crayon" (the artist) and "La Plume" (the writer). "Le Crayon" states that he will no longer illustrate that which "La Plume" creates. Instead, the artist will create what he desires. The writer agrees to then provide the text.

The artist is Jean Ignace Isadore Gérard, called J. J. Grandville (1803-1847), and this work is his undisputed masterpiece. *Un autre monde* was first brought out in thirty-six installments in 1843. Yet it was only with the final installment that the writer's name was finally revealed. "La Plume" was in fact Taxile Delord (1815-1877), who would also provide the text for Grandville's next two projects and later become editor-in-chief of the journal *Charivari*.

Delord's vapid text tells of three neo-gods—Dr. Puff, Krackq, and Hahblle—who set out to explore the earth, the sea, and the sky. What they find, of course, is the bizarre universe created by Grandville. On earth, the vegetable world conspires to free itself from the human appetite. In the sea, a ball takes place in which animals masquerade as human beings. And in the sky, a solar eclipse is revealed to be a kiss shared by the Sun and the Moon, who are husband and wife. In short, Grandville animated the entire physical world. In the words of Baudelaire, "with super-human courage, this man devoted his life to refashioning creation."[1]

It is not hard to imagine Grandville's influence on the later work of the Surrealists, or even Walt Disney. But perhaps the most obvious influence can be seen in Lewis Carroll's *Alice's Adventures in Wonderland* (1865).[2] Witness the illustration entitled *La bataille des cartes*, depicting one of the many hallucinations which come to Hahblle in chapter 32, "Les métamorphoses du sommeil." In this vision, Grandville animated the hearts, spades, diamonds, and clubs, who have jumped out of the plane of the playing card itself. Carroll would later animate the entire deck.

S.R.

LA BATAILLE DES CARTES.

34. WILLIAM MAKEPEACE
THACKERAY

Vanity Fair, a novel without a
hero . . . with illustrations on steel
and wood by the author. London:
Bradbury and Evans, 1847-1848.
Original 20 monthly parts in 19.
Disregarding advertisements: parts
1 to 18 each with 32 p., [2] leaves of
plates; part 19/20 with 48, xvi p.,
[4] leaves of plates. All essential
points of the first issue.[1] Page size:
8¾ x 5⅝ in. (222 x 143 mm.)
Binding: Original printed yellow
wrappers in full blue morocco solander
case. Signature of John McConnell on
3 of the wrappers. Robert Sterling
Clark Collection.

ILLUSTRATIONS: Frontispiece, added
title page, and 38 plates etched by
Thackeray; 66 historiated initials and
84 wood-engraved vignettes after
Thackeray.

REFERENCES: Van Duzer 230.

NOTES:

1. Van Duzer, p. 132, lists the essential
   points of the first issue.

2. For a brief but highly informative
   survey of Thackeray's career as an
   illustrator, see John Buchanan-Brown,
   *The Illustrations of William Makepeace
   Thackeray* (North Pomfret, Vt.: David
   and Charles, Inc., 1979).

Thackeray (1811-1863) began both his artistic and his literary careers in a rather aimless and unfocused fashion.[2] Having left Cambridge University in 1830 after only one year, he spent most of the next few years on the Continent enjoying himself immensely but studying art and literature only a little. His early attempts at employment as a Paris correspondent for London papers met with little success and his search for opportunities as an illustrator met with even less. By the late 1830s, however, Thackeray's parallel careers in journalism and illustration had begun to take shape.

When the first monthly installment of *Vanity Fair* came out in January 1847, Thackeray had already become well known for his fiction and criticism in *Fraser's Magazine* and for his humorous pieces and satirical cartoons in *Punch*. In his contributions to these periodicals, and in the few small books he had managed to publish before *Vanity Fair* appeared, Thackeray demonstrated his powers of observation, particularly of people. This quality is to be found throughout *Vanity Fair*, in which any number of characters are sketched in word and picture with wit, sympathy, and, above all, candor.

Thackeray's graphic style, with its immediacy and directness, is perfectly suited to the novelist's literary style. Throughout *Vanity Fair* the ingenious initials augment the text's implication that humor is to be found in everyday, human drama. In one initial, the fragment of a ladder in an elopement scene serves as the *H*; in another, the *O* is a ship's porthole; and in a third (on p. 232), the clown's stilts make a *W*. The full-page etchings and the vignettes guide the reader's visualization of characters and events that might be only briefly described in the novel. For example, Mrs. Peggy O'Dowd is portrayed as stout, jolly, and dressed in a riding habit when she first meets Amelia. But Thackeray's illustration (p. 233) gives us a great deal more by emphasizing the very different shapes of the two women. In addition, the quick, simple strokes underscore the lively and conversational tone of the text. It is no wonder that Thackeray's illustrations are widely enjoyed for their economy, clarity, and humanity.

J.D.W.

CHAPTER XXVII.

IN WHICH AMELIA JOINS HER REGIMENT.

HEN Jos's fine carriage drove up to the inn door at Chatham, the first face which Amelia recognized was the friendly countenance of Captain Dobbin, who had been pacing the street for an hour past in expectation of his friends' arrival. The Captain, with shells on his frock-coat, and a crimson sash and sabre, presented a military appearance, which made Jos quite proud to be able to claim such an acquaintance, and the stout civilian hailed him with a cordiality very different from the reception which Jos vouchsafed to his friends in Brighton and Bond Street.

Along with the Captain was Ensign Stubble; who, as the barouche neared the inn, burst out with an exclamation of "By Jove! what a pretty girl!" highly applauding Osborne's choice. Indeed, Amelia dressed in her wedding-pelisse and pink ribbons, with a flush in her face, occasioned by rapid travel through the open air, looked so fresh and pretty, as fully to justify the Ensign's compliment. Dobbin liked him for making it. As he stepped forward to help the lady out of the carriage, Stubble saw what a pretty little hand she gave him, and what a sweet pretty little foot came tripping down the step. He blushed profusely, and made the very best bow of which he was capable; to which Amelia, seeing the number of the —th regiment embroidered on the Ensign's cap, replied with a blushing smile, and a curtsey on her part; which finished the young Ensign on the spot. Dobbin took most kindly to Mr. Stubble from that day, and encouraged him to talk about Amelia in their private walks, and at each other's quarters. It became the fashion indeed among all the honest young fellows of the —th to adore and admire Mrs. Osborne. Her simple artless behaviour, and modest kindness of demeanour, won all their unsophisticated hearts; all which simplicity and sweetness are quite impossible to describe in print. But who has not beheld these among women, and recognized the presence of all sorts of qualities in them, even though they say no more to you than that they are engaged to dance the next quadrille, or that it is very hot weather? George, always the champion of his regiment, rose immensely

in the opinion of the youth of the corps, by his gallantry in marrying this portionless young creature, and by his choice of such a pretty kind partner.

In the sitting-room which was awaiting the travellers, Amelia, to her surprise, found a letter addressed to Mrs. Captain Osborne. It was a triangular billet, on pink paper, and sealed with a dove and an olive branch, and a profusion of light-blue sealing wax, and it was written in a very large, though undecided female hand.

"It's Peggy O'Dowd's fist," said George, laughing. "I know it by the kisses on the seal." And in fact, it was a note from Mrs. Major O'Dowd, requesting the pleasure of Mrs. Osborne's company that very evening to a small friendly party. "You must go," George said. "You will make acquaintance with the regiment there. O'Dowd goes in command of the regiment, and Peggy goes in command of O'Dowd."

But they had not been for many minutes in the enjoyment of Mrs. O'Dowd's letter, when the door was flung open, and a stout jolly lady, in a riding-habit, followed by a couple of officers of Ours, entered the room.

35. HONORÉ DE BALZAC

Les contes drolatiques, colligez ez abbayes de Touraine, et mis en lumière par le sieur de Balzac pour l'esbattement des pantagruelistes et non aultres. Cinquiesme édition, illustrée de 425 dessins par Gustave Doré. Paris: Bureaux de la Société générale de librairie, 1855. xxxi, [1], 614, [1] p. Page size: 8⅛ x 5 in. (206 x 127 mm.) Binding: Full green morocco gilt, by Cuzin. Robert Sterling Clark Collection.

ILLUSTRATIONS: 425 vignettes, head- and tailpieces after Doré, engraved on wood by Lavielle, Riault, and others.

REFERENCES: Carteret 48-56; Ray 244.

NOTES:

1. Nigel Gosling, *Gustave Doré* (Newton Abbot, England: David & Charles, 1973), 18.
2. John Ruskin, *The Works of John Ruskin*, ed. E. T. Cook and Alexander Wedderburn (London: George Allen; New York: Longmans, Green, 1950), 17, 344.

Les contes drolatiques, by Honoré de Balzac (1799-1850), first appeared as three installments of ten tales each in the years 1832, 1833, and 1837. Writing in the style of Rabelais, Balzac presented a pastiche of medieval France, adopting a pseudo-medieval language to relate these ribald tales of fallen nuns, gallant crusaders, and corrupt officials who populate the town of Touraine. These stories were immensely popular and provided Balzac with an income while he continued writing the more ambitious novels which constitute his *La comédie humaine*.

Gustave Doré (1832-1883) began his career as an illustrator at the early age of fifteen when he found employment at the *Journal pour rire*. And he had just illustrated Rabelais's *Oeuvres* (Paris, 1854) when he was offered the commission to illustrate this edition of Balzac's tales. Particularly suited to the task, Doré is purported to have produced the 425 drawings in two weeks' time.[1] These illustrations would secure his reputation as the leading book illustrator of the era.

Doré was the last of the Romantics, and his illustrations for Balzac's tales are packed with the full range of Romantic imagery. The landscape is dark, often sinister, the character portraits are grotesque, and the battle scenes are full of decapitations and dismemberments in vivid detail. One of his more macabre illustrations, shown here, is for the tale "Le Succube" and depicts the act of necrophilism, just one of many evils of which a young moorish woman has been wrongly accused.

But Doré remained faithful to the text; his imagination was very sympathetic to that of Balzac. Perhaps no one can relate their kindred spirit better than their most disapproving critic, John Ruskin, who said that "both text and illustrations are as powerful as it is ever in the nature of evil things to be. . . . Nothing more witty, nor more inventively horrible, has yet to be produced in the evil literature, or by the evil art, of man. . . ."[2]

The publishers must have anticipated the success of this edition, for the initial printing was of ten thousand copies. In addition, they produced a deluxe edition, printed on *papier du chine* and limited to twenty-five copies. The Clark copy is one of these very rare copies in which the quality of the engravings is exceptionally fine.

S.R.

Plusieurs l'avoyent veue, durant la nuict, aller ez cimetières, y
gruger de ieunes morts, pour ce que elle ne pouvoyt assouvir
aultrement le diable qui trépignoyt dedans ses entrailles et s'y
demenoyt comme ung oraige.

36. OWEN JONES

The Grammar of Ornament, by Owen Jones, illustrated by examples from various styles of ornament. . . . London: Day and Son, 1856. 111 p. in various pagings, [101] leaves of plates. Page size: 22 x 14¹¹⁄₁₆ in. (559 x 373 mm.) Binding: Publisher's ½ brown morocco. Stamp of Jos. Bell DeRemme, Architect. Gift of Mary Ann Beinecke.

ILLUSTRATIONS: Chromolithographed title page and 100 chromolithographed plates after Jones by Francis Bedford; numerous wood-engraved vignettes after Jones.

REFERENCES: Friedman 151-152; Ray 1976, 228.

NOTES:

1. Owen Jones, *The Grammar of Ornament*, 4.

2. Ibid., 2.

The beautiful plates in this encyclopedia of ornament represent a high point in the history of chromolithography. Developed barely fifty years before the publication of *The Grammar of Ornament*, lithography flourished as a result of its contact with early Victorian technology but fell into disuse at the end of the century with the advent of photomechanical processes for color reproduction. During the heyday of chromolithography, skilled draftsmen such as Francis Bedford and high-quality printing firms such as Day and Son were in great demand. Only twenty years earlier Owen Jones (1809-1874), then a young architect, had to set up his own printing establishment to print the illustrations for his first book, *Plans, Elevations, Sections, and Details of the Alhambra* (London, 1836-1845).

In this book, and in the many others for which Jones provided designs, the colored plates are characterized by flat, opaque colors with discrete boundaries. This style, while it might place great demands on the draftsman and printer who had to insure that the colors, each printed from a separate surface, were properly registered, emphasized the decorative qualities of the subject. In *The Grammar of Ornament* Jones, whose major architectural achievements were associated with the ornament of surfaces in large public buildings, capitalized on chromolithography's potential for reproducing flat patterns.

A significant feature of this work is the large number of styles represented and the theoretical issues raised by their apparent diversity. Jones included ornament from "savage tribes" along with examples from Egypt, the Near East, Asia (except Japan, which was still almost unknown in the West), and Europe from ancient Greece to seventeenth-century Italy. In addition to the one hundred spectacular plates and the descriptive texts (some of which were written by his friends John O. Westwood, John Barley Waring, and Mathew Digby Wyatt) accompanying each section of *The Grammar of Ornament*, Jones also provided a preface and list of thirty-seven propositions which he described as "principles in the arrangement of form and colour . . . advocated throughout this work."[1] The book, then, had a pedagogical purpose and was not simply a compendium of ornaments drawn from many cultures and ages. In fact, the diversity of styles was part of Jones's point, for he stressed that great ornament is based on very few laws, all of which may be gleaned from the "landmarks" in his book.[2]

One cannot help but be impressed with the scope and scale of Jones's work. The text is authoritative, there are close to twenty different styles represented, and in the one hundred plates there are several thousand details of ornament illustrated. Above all, the sheer beauty and complexity of the plates (that shown here, pl. 86, contains twenty-two different Italian designs of the sixteenth and seventeenth centuries) make *The Grammar of Ornament* a masterpiece of color illustration.

J.D.W.

ITALIAN N° 1.

37. Jean Anthelme
Brillat-Savarin

Physiologie du gout, précédée d'une notice par Alp. Karr; dessins de Bertall. Paris: Furne et cie., 1864. [6], 459, [1] p., [7] leaves of plates, plus publisher's catalogue (4 p.). Page size: 10⅛ x 6⅝ in. (258 x 169 mm.) Binding: ¾ blue morocco gilt. Robert Sterling Clark Collection.

ILLUSTRATIONS: Frontispiece and 6 full-page plates printed on *chine collé*, engraved by Geoffroy after Bertall, and 245 wood-engraved vignettes, initials, head- and tailpieces, engraved by Riault, Midderigh, and others after Bertall. Original wood-engraved wrappers with 2 vignettes after Bertall bound in.

REFERENCES: Brivois 65-66; Carteret 108; Vicaire I, 928.[1]

NOTES:

1. Brivois and Carteret describe in detail the 1848 edition, with only a brief mention of the 1864 edition. Vicaire describes the 1864 edition in more detail, yet does not list the number of plates. The 1848 edition has a total of eight plates, one of which is a portrait of Brillat-Savarin. This plate was not included in the 1864 edition.

2. Brillat-Savarin, *The Physiology of Taste*, trans. M.F.K. Fisher (San Francisco: North Point Press, 1986), 3.

3. Ibid., 12.

"Tell me what you eat, and I shall tell you what you are."[2] So reads the most quoted aphorism set forth by Jean Anthelme Brillat-Savarin (1755-1826) in his *Physiologie du goût*. In addition to providing a series of eminently quotable aphorisms, Brillat-Savarin's gastronomic classic takes the form of "Meditations" on various culinary subjects, such as appetite, thirst, digestion, and bouquet. These are followed by "Varieties," a series of anecdotes and recipes. Brillat-Savarin was a lawyer by vocation, and when he first published *Physiologie du goût*, in 1825, it was at his own expense. In addition, he published it anonymously, attributing the work to "a Professor."[3] However, it was enormously successful and immediately appeared in numerous editions, often illustrated.

Among the various artists to illustrate Brillat-Savarin's book was Albert d'Arnoux (1820-1882), known as Bertall, a pseudonym (and anagram of his given name) suggested to him by Balzac. Bertall was a prolific illustrator, providing designs in the Romantic tradition for, among others, Balzac's *Petites misères de la vie conjugale* (Paris, 1845). He was also a caricaturist and frequent contributor to the journals *Illustration* and *Journal pour rire*.

Bertall's illustrations for Brillat-Savarin's *Physiologie du goût* first appeared in an edition published by Gabriel de Gonet in 1848. The Clark copy is from an edition published by Furne in 1864 containing the same illustrations, with some variation. Shown here is one of the full-page plates, engraved on steel, which accompanies two of Brillat-Savarin's "Meditations": one on obesity and one on thinness. Instead of illustrating the author's amusing anecdotes, Bertall invented his own. For example, near the center is an image of a rotund gentleman astride a horse who has collapsed under the strain of such enormous weight. And at the lower left is his vision of a spindly woman whose body is barely visible underneath her contoured (and padded) undergarment.

Bertall's wit is also obvious in his comic headpieces and initials, which were engraved on wood. In his design for the headpiece accompanying the "Meditation" on obesity, Bertall imagined a whole family (including the pet pig) with so much fat that they no longer have the use of their legs; their balloon-shaped bodies simply roll or bounce about. On this same page, he made creative use of the two semi-circular voids formed by the initial letter *S*, into which he stuffed the hefty paunches of two plump gentlemen.

S.R.

L'OBÉSITÉ ET LA MAIGREUR

38. LUDOVIC HALÉVY

La famille Cardinal. Paris: Calmann Lévy, 1883. [4], 210, [1] p. No. 36 of 50 copies printed on "papier du Japon." Page size: 6¹⁵⁄₁₆ x 5⅞ in. (178 x 144 mm.) Binding: Full blue morocco gilt and red morocco gilt doublures with ribbed silk and marbled paper flyleaves, by Mercier. Bookplate of Robert Hoe. Robert Sterling Clark Collection.

ILLUSTRATIONS: Original watercolors on half title, frontispiece, and 198 pages by Henriot. Autograph on half title reads "Croquis d'Henriot, 1893."

REFERENCES: The Clark copy is unique.

The primary interest in this book lies in its inception, for it was created for the bibliophile's delight. In the late nineteenth century several bibliographic societies were established, and book collectors became preoccupied with all aspects of book production. When Calmann Lévy published this book in a limited edition of fifty copies, he chose especially fine paper and printed the text in small blocks, leaving wide margins so that the collector could commission illustrations from an artist of his own choosing. Perhaps it was the renowned bibliophile Robert Hoe (1839-1909) who commissioned these illustrations. The volume bears his bookplate, and his activities in various bibliophilic societies sustain such a supposition.

In any case, illustrations for this copy of Halévy's *La famille Cardinal* were commissioned from Henri Maigrot, known as Henriot (1857-1933). Henriot was a draftsman, caricaturist, and author. His caricatures appeared in the journal *Illustration* and, in 1890, he became director of the journal *Charivari*. As an illustrator he provided compositions for, among others, Guy de Maupaussant's *Imprudence* (Paris, 1899) and Ludovic Halévy's *Karikari* (Paris, 1887).

Ludovic Halévy (1834-1908) is known primarily as a librettist who collaborated with Henri Meilhac on Jacques Offenbach's *La Belle Hélène* and other operettas. But he was also a successful novelist. His most popular novel was *La famille Cardinal*, which relates lively scenes from the life of a lower-class Parisian family. It was published in many editions and was illustrated by many artists, including Edgar Degas.

For this copy of *La famille Cardinal*, Henriot filled the margins with entertaining images, first sketching in pencil a vague outline of the composition, then painting in blocks of color, and finally completing the composition by over-drawing the outlines, details, and shadowings in black ink. This technique is clearly seen on pages 140, 154, 159, and especially on page 59, where no color was used. His use of the page was extremely creative. In one instance, he turned the text block into the words appearing on an old vellum charter by drawing a ragged outline around the text and filling in with an ochre-colored wash (p. 26). In another illustration, a ladder is hiding underneath the text block, its two legs extending into the lower left and right margins. A man and a woman, having climbed from opposing sides, meet at the top of the ladder, which appears in the top margin (p. 188). And on the double-page spread shown here (pp. 202-203), Henriot has filled nearly all of the marginal areas with a brilliant display of fireworks, illustrating the final dramatic scene in Halévy's novel, when the sky was to be lit up with the message "A bas les jésuites" instead of "Vive l'empereur."

S.R.

un effet énorme et, à neuf heures et
demie, on descend au jardin pour le feu
d'artifice. Cela commence par marcher ad-
mirablement. Fusées, flammes de Bengale,
feux tournants, fontaines jaillissantes, rien
ne rate; et, vous savez, ordinairement, il y
a toujours un tas de choses qui ratent dans
les feux d'artifice. Le temps était à souhait :
pas de lune et pas de vent. Tout à coup,
voilà qu'une construction de feu s'élève
dans les arbres... C'était la pièce montée.
On voit se dessiner des colonnes, une porte.
Tout le monde disait : « Ah! que c'est
beau ! Comme c'est mieux que chez le
maire ! »

« — Attendez! leur criait Monsieur Car-
» dinal, attendez, ce n'est rien encore!...
» Attendez le fronton !... Attendez l'inscrip-
» tion !... »

» Il se dresse, le fronton; elle s'allume,
l'inscription, mais quelle horreur ! Savez-vous
ce qui s'écrit en lettres de feu au haut du

fronton, au lieu de : *A bas les jésuites!* Ce
qui s'écrit, c'est :

VIVE L'EMPEREUR !

» Comment est-ce arrivé ? Je n'en sais
rien encore. Était-ce une plaisanterie du
petit prince, qui se serait amusé à nous
envoyer un feu d'artifice bonapartiste, à la
place d'un feu d'artifice anticlérical? Je ne
peux pas croire cela de la part d'un jeune
homme si distingué et si amoureux de
Pauline. Était-ce une erreur de M. Rug-
gieri ? C'est une très grande maison
dans laquelle il doit y avoir des feux d'artifice pour toutes les opinions. Ils ont pu se
tromper de nuance. Peut-être aussi ont-ils
essayé d'écouler un vieux rossignol qu'ils
avaient en magasin ! Bien des feux d'artifice ont dû leur rester pour compte au moment de la chute de l'Empire. Ça ne serait
pas délicat de leur part, et même, en y
pensant, ce n'est pas admissible, car ils

39. ADOLPHE JULLIEN

Hector Berlioz; sa vie et ses oeuvres, ouvrage orné de quatorze lithographies originales par M. Fantin-Latour, de douze portraits de Hector Berlioz, de trois planches hors texte et de 122 gravures, scènes théâtrales, caricatures, portraits d'artistes, autographes, etc. Paris: Librairie de l'art, 1888. xvi, 386, [2] p., [17] leaves of plates. Page size: 12½ x 9 in. (315 x 230 mm.) Binding: Modern marbled paper boards. Purchase 1988.

ILLUSTRATIONS: 14 full-page lithographed plates by Fantin-Latour printed on *chine collé*, 1 etched and 2 gravure plates, and 122 wood-engraved and process illustrations after various artists.

REFERENCES: Ray 370; Vicaire 615-616.

NOTES:

1. Douglas Druick and Michel Hoag, *Fantin-Latour* (Ottawa: National Gallery of Canada, 1983), 279.

2. Ibid., 219-233.

3. Adolphe Jullien, *Fantin-Latour: sa vie et ses amitiés* (Paris: Lucien Laveur, 1909).

Henri Fantin-Latour (1836-1904) has been identified with nearly all of the movements of late nineteenth-century French art. His circle of friends included the Impressionists—Degas, Monet, Renoir—but his art remained relatively untouched by their experiments. His well-known portraits and still lifes, especially those of flowers, are solidly within the tradition of Realism. But he also produced imaginary subjects, packed with allegory, which at once recall the Romanticism of Delacroix and parallel the Symbolism of Gustave Moreau.

For the most part, Fantin-Latour's imaginary subjects were inspired by music. Richard Wagner's music was the most influential source, but Fantin-Latour also illustrated subjects from the music of Berlioz, Brahms, Rossini, Schumann, and Weber. And while these projects included large-scale paintings, they were far more successful in the medium of lithography. In fact, Fantin-Latour is given credit for having revived interest in this art,[1] which by the 1870s had been largely abandoned in favor of etching and wood engraving.

For Jullien's monograph on the Romantic composer Hector Berlioz, Fantin-Latour created fourteen lithographs which illustrate scenes from the operatic and choral work of Berlioz. A few of the plates are later versions of compositions which had been previously issued. Such is the case with the final plate, entitled *Apothéose*, which has a long history. Fantin-Latour first conceived of an homage to Berlioz during a performance of the composer's *Roméo et Juliette* in 1875. Within days he was at work on a composition which first appeared as a lithograph entitled *L'anniversaire*. The following year he translated the composition onto canvas and exhibited *L'anniversaire* at the salon.[2]

In each manifestation, the components remain essentially the same. In the background is the tomb of Berlioz, over which an angel (from the oratorio *L'enfance du Christ*) is placing a garland. Below the angel, offering a wreath and a bough, are Marguerite (*La damnation de Faust*) and Dido (*Les Troyens*). In front are Romeo, Juliet, and a contemporary figure of a man. In the center is the muse Clio who points to Berlioz's name with one hand and with the other holds a scroll which lists his finest works. Finally, to the left is the weeping muse of music.

The author of the text is Adolphe Jullien (1845-1932), a music critic and friend of Fantin-Latour. In 1886 Fantin-Latour had provided fourteen lithographs for Jullien's study of Richard Wagner. And in 1909 Jullien published one of the first monographs devoted to Henri Fantin-Latour.[3]

S.R.

40. LOUIS MAURICE
    BOUTET DE MONVEL

Jeanne d'Arc, par M. Boutet de
Monvel. Paris, E. Plon, Nourrit &
cie., [1896]. [78] leaves of plates.
"Exemplaire papier du Japon,
no. 53." Page size: 13¼ x 16¾ in.
(342 x 432 mm.) Binding: ½ purple
morocco. Robert Sterling Clark
Collection.

ILLUSTRATIONS: 48 color lithographed plates by Boutet de Monvel,
paginated according to the trade
edition and mounted on heavy paper.
Bound in (and mounted on a lighter
stock paper) are 30 trial proofs without text. Of these, 27 were printed
on clay-coated paper and 3 were
printed on *papier du chine*. Each proof
has registration holes on either side of
the image, and several bear the
printers' signatures, Ducourtioux and
Huillard.

REFERENCES: Carteret 1946 IV, 79;
Ray 365.

NOTES:
1. A revealing work on Boutet de Monvel
   as artist, especially on his *Jeanne
   d'Arc*, its production, states of plates,
   etc., is Ann Van Devanter Townsend,
   *Maurice Boutet de Monvel: Master of
   French Illustration and Portraiture*
   (Washington, D.C.: The Trust for
   Museum Exhibitions, 1987).

The legend of Joan of Arc has captivated audiences for centuries. Joan's story began with her visions in which saints appointed her as saviour of France, for whom the Hundred Years' War was going badly. In short, Joan rallied the French troops and led them to victories at Orléans, Patay, and numerous other battles, thus allowing the Dauphin Charles to be crowned King Charles VII. Joan continued to expel the enemy from France, but without the support of the throne, who no longer needed her and neglected to come to her aid when she was eventually captured by Burgundians. She was sold to the English, tried for heresy, and burned at the stake in 1431. Her story, symbolizing faith, patriotism, courage, and hope, has been told in countless versions and has appeared in numerous editions published for children.

Louis Maurice Boutet de Monvel (1850-1913) was one of the leading illustrators of children's books in nineteenth-century France. He was trained as a painter and known also as one of the leading portraitists of children. For his version of the legend of Joan of Arc, Boutet de Monvel wrote the text as well as provided the illustrations. Published in 1896, *Jeanne d'Arc* became his most highly praised work. The illustrations, drawn in a stylized manner, are nevertheless rich in detail and ornament and were printed in subtle, flat colors, characteristic of his work in general.

The deluxe Japan paper copies of *Jeanne d'Arc* were issued in portfolios with each page separately mounted on large paper, and because the Clark copy has been bound, it is impossible to fully appreciate the numerous illustrations which should appear on facing pages. Shown here, for example, is the illustration of the battle of Patay, which actually begins on the previous page. The horse's head which extends into the left margin helps connect the two pages. It is possible, however, to appreciate Boutet de Monvel's idealization of the story. Here is Joan on the lead horse in the background, carrying a banner and wearing a flowing robe over her armor. But while she is leading the troops into a battle portrayed with great exuberance, the illustration conveys little evidence of the battle's brutality.

The Clark copy also contains several proofs of the illustrations printed before the text was added. Three of these are printed on *papier du chine*, on which the colors appear brighter but still retain their flatness.[1] It is no wonder that Boutet de Monvel's influence on the illustration of children's books extended well into the twentieth century.

S.R.

Le 18 juin, Jeanne atteignit, près de Patay, l'armée anglaise conduite par Talbot et Falstaff.

« En nom Dieu il faut les combattre, dit-elle ; quand ils seraient pendus aux nues, nous les aurons, parce que Dieu nous les envoie pour que nous les châtiions. Notre gentil Roi aura aujourd'hui la plus grande victoire qu'il eut. » Elle voulait se porter à l'avant-garde, on la retint, et La Hire fut chargé d'attaquer les Anglais pour les obliger à faire volte-face, afin de donner aux troupes françaises le temps d'arriver. Mais l'attaque de La Hire fut si impétueuse que tout céda devant lui. Lorsque Jeanne accourut avec ses hommes d'armes, les Anglais se retiraient en désordre. Leur retraite devint une fuite. Talbot fut pris.

« Vous ne pensiez pas ce matin que cela vous arriverait », lui dit le duc d'Alençon. « C'est la fortune de la guerre », répondit Talbot.

41. LONGUS

Les pastorales de Longus, ou
Daphnis et Chloé, traduction de
Messire J. Amyot . . . revue, corrigée,
complétée de nouveau, refaits en
grande partie par Paul-Louis
Courier . . . lithographies originales
de P. Bonnard. Paris: Ambroise
Vollard, 1902. x, 294, [3] p. One of
200 copies on Van Gelder bearing the
watermark "Daphnis et Chloé." Page
size: 12 x 9⅝ in. (303 x 245 mm.)
Binding: Full green morocco gilt, by
Stierli. Purchase 1989.

ILLUSTRATIONS: Lithographed title-
page vignette, 143 lithographed
⅔-page vignettes, 11 lithographed
head- and tailpieces, and 1 lithographed decoration (title page verso)
by Bonnard, printed by Auguste Clot.

REFERENCES: Ray 384; Skira 22.

NOTES:

1. For more information on Vollard's
activity as a publisher, see Una
E. Johnson, *Ambroise Vollard, Editeur:
Prints, Books, Bronzes* (New York:
Museum of Modern Art, 1977).

The well-known Parisian art dealer and print publisher Ambroise Vollard (1865-1939) was also one of the earliest patrons and publishers of *livres d'artistes*. His initial offering was an edition of the poet Verlaine's *Parallèlement* (1900), for which he commissioned lithographs from Pierre Bonnard (1867-1947). This work was a commercial failure, with critics condemning both Bonnard's free compositional style—his illustrations floated throughout the margins and in and out of the text—and even his use of lithography in an era when the bibliophiles preferred woodcut illustrations. However, Vollard persisted in his venture; over the next forty years he continued to publish deluxe editions illustrated by, among others, Raoul Dufy, Maurice Denis, Odilon Redon, and Pablo Picasso.

In 1902 Vollard's second offering appeared, again illustrated by Bonnard. This time Vollard chose the ever-popular pastoral *Daphnis et Chloé*, by Longus, which had a long tradition of illustration in France (see cat. no. 14 for an early eighteenth-century edition and cat. no. 42 for another twentieth-century edition). Similarly, Bonnard chose to contain his images within a traditional, rectangular format. The book was only slightly more successful than *Parallèlement*, yet today both are considered among the best ever published by Vollard.

Daphnis et Chloé displays all of the characteristics of Vollard's *deluxe* editions: the roman typeface was carefully chosen, in this instance printed in the same ink as the illustrations; the paper was especially prepared, bearing the watermark "Daphnis et Chloé"; and the illustrations were printed with extreme care, in this case by Auguste Clot, who was a master of the technique of lithography.[1]

Though today Bonnard is known primarily as a painter, his early successes were indeed in the graphic arts. He was a member of the Nabis, a circle of artists with whom he shared the desire to extend the decorative qualities of the art of painting. As is evident in his illustrations for *Daphnis et Chloé*, Bonnard was a superb draftsman whose freely composed images transferred well into lithographs. The illustration, shown here, of Daphnis swimming nude appears to be sketched right onto the page. This spontaneous quality perfectly captures the innocence and unabashed sensuality of Longus's pastoral.

S.R.

dans la caverne; si accouroit incontinent et, lui
ôtant sa couronne qu'il baisoit d'abord, se la mettoit
sur la tête, et elle, pendant qu'il se baignoit tout nu,
prenoit sa robe et se la vêtoit, la baisant aussi pre-
mièrement. Tantôt ils s'entre-jetoient des pommes,

Les pastorales de Longus, ou **Daphnis & Chloé**; version d'Amyot, revue et complétée par P.-L. Courier; bois originaux d'Aristide Maillol. Paris: Les Frères Gonin, 1937. 217, [4] p. No. 345 of 500 copies printed on "papier Maillol" and signed by the artist. Page size: 8¾ x 5¾ in. (223 x 144 mm.) In printed wrappers, as issued. Purchase 1988.

ILLUSTRATIONS: 48 woodcut text illustrations and 18 woodcut initials by Maillol, printed in black by Phillipe Gonin.

REFERENCES: Skira 216.

NOTES:

1. John Rewald, *The Woodcuts of Aristide Maillol* (New York: Pantheon, 1951), xxvi-xxvii.

Aristide Maillol (1861-1944) is best known for his sculpture, but he began his career as a painter and tapestry maker. In the last decade of the nineteenth century he was influenced by the woodcuts of Paul Gauguin and tried his hand at the traditional, black-line technique. He produced only seven prints between 1893 and 1900 and did not return to the technique until 1912, when he began to work on his first illustrated book, an edition of Virgil's *Eclogues*. Published in 1926, the work was so successful that Maillol was convinced to continue his career in illustration in addition to sculpting.

Daphnis & Chloé was the fourth book illustrated by Maillol, and, like so many before him, he found inspiration in this pastoral by the Greek writer Longus (see cat. nos. 14 and 41 for earlier examples). As John Rewald noted, Maillol "selected undramatic episodes . . . or reduced the dramatic content" for his illustrations. Rewald also pointed out that the image shown here, which depicts Daphnis having picked an apple for Chloé, has been illustrated by others who chose a moment earlier in the episode, when Daphnis climbed to the top of the tree to obtain this, the last apple.[1] This image also bears witness to Maillol's serene, classically inspired style.

Phillipe Gonin printed *Daphnis & Chloé* in both French and English language editions, the latter for the London publisher A. Zwemmer. Maillol worked very closely with Gonin, playing, as always, a major role in the book's production. Maillol was particularly concerned with the quality of paper for his books and had earlier established a mill outside of Paris to manufacture new papers. The *papier Maillol* produced for *Daphnis & Chloé* bears a beautiful watermark which is a typical, classical nude designed by Maillol.

S.R.

foi de laboureur, que Chloé jamais ne seroit
à autre que lui. DAPHNIS aussitôt, sans
vouloir ni boire ni manger, s'en recourut
vers elle, et l'ayant trouvée qui tiroit ses
brebis et faisoit des fromages, il lui annonça
la bonne nouvelle de leur futur mariage,
et de là en avant ne feignoit de la baiser
devant tout le monde, comme sa fiancée,
et l'aider en toutes ses besognes, tiroit les
brebis dans les seilles, faisoit prendre le

163

INDEXES

(AUTHORS AND ARTISTS, PROVENANCE, BINDERS)

Racine, Jean Baptiste, 1639-1699, 15,
62
Raffet, Auguste, 1804-1860, 19
Robert, Hubert, 1733-1808, 72
Saint-Aubin, Augustin de, 1736-1807,
54
Saint-Non, Jean Claude Richard de,
1727-1791, 72
Salomon, Bernard, 1506/1510-1561,
15, 36
Schedel, Hartmann, 1440-1514, 14, 28
Sève, Jacques de, act. 1742-1788, 62
Strang, William, 1859-1921, 21
Surtees, Robert Smith, 1805-1864, 13
Tenniel, Sir John, 1820-1914, 20, 21
Thackeray, William Makepeace,
1811-1863, 20, 94
Thompson, Charles, 1791-1843, 86
Thomson, James, 1700-1748, 80
Tomkins, Peltro William, 1760-1840,
80
Torelli, Giacomo, 1604/1608-1678,
15, 46
Tory, Geoffroy de, c. 1480-1533, 30
Townsend, Frederick Henry,
1868-1920, 21
Vernet, Horace, 1789-1863, 18
Virgil, 70-19 B.C., 14
Wallhausen, Jean Jacques de,
17th century, 13
Woeiriot, Jacquemin, act. 1503-1533,
30
Wolgemut, Michael, 1434-1519, 14,
28

PROVENANCE

Barbet, L. A., 15
Beinecke, Mary Ann, 98
Bishop, Cortlandt Field, 15, 18, 20
Davignon, William, 38
Debure, Guillaume, 54
DeRemme, Jos. Bell, 98
EHLK, 52
Este, Hippolyte d', 12, 13
Giraud, Charles, 48
Grolier, Jean, 14
Heredia, Ricardo, 28
Hoe, Robert, 20, 74, 102
Honywood, Ph[ilip], of Marks Hall, 40
Huth, Henry, 13, 14
Kern, Jerome, 13
Juynboll, W. R., 72
La Vieuville, Marquis de, 32
Loo, Pierre van, 18
Louis XVI, 54
Lys, Dumoulin du, 68
McConnell, John, 94
Monin, L. M., 32
Moura, Edouard, 17
Nossam, Robert, 92
Parker, R. Townley, 52
Perrevine, Anne de, 32
Pozzo, Gio. Pietro, 36
Rahir, Edouard, 15, 17, 32, 44, 48
Rattier, Léon, 17
Saint-Amand, J. P., Chevalier de, 15
Séguier, Pierre, 15
Sully, Maximilien de Béthune, duc de, 15
Tasso, Torquato, 13
Tatton, Reginald Arthur, 52
Thornhill, J[ames], 34
Toulouse, Louis Alexandre de Bourbon,
comte de, 48
Vieillard, Jacques, 84

BINDERS